From our Kitchen to Yours

# Simple Savory Meals

**Our favorite recipes for easy-to-prepare meals, using your favorite cuts of meat**

*To everyday cooks who love to serve tasty meals to family & friends!*

Gooseberry Patch
An imprint of Globe Pequot
246 Goose Lane
Guilford, CT 06437

**www.gooseberrypatch.com**
**1 800 854 6673**

••••••••••••••••••••

Do you have a tried & true recipe... tip, craft or memory that you'd like to see featured in a **Gooseberry Patch** cookbook? Please visit our website at www.gooseberrypatch.com and follow the easy steps to submit your favorite family recipe.

Or send them to us at:
Gooseberry Patch
PO Box 812
Columbus, OH 43216-0812

Don't forget to include the number of servings your recipe makes, plus your name, address, phone number and email address. If we select your recipe, your name will appear right along with it... and you'll receive a FREE copy of the book!

# CONTENTS

# Simple Savory Meal Tips

Whether you're fixing a simple soup supper or a full-course dinner, getting a delicious, wholesome meal on the table has never been easier! These days, everyday cooks have lots of quick-fix meal ideas that make it a snap to whip up tasty dishes without a lot of fuss.

**We've gathered some of our essential cooking tips that help make dinner prep easier:**

• A full pantry makes it so easy to toss together all kinds of tasty meals in a jiffy. Stock the cupboard with cans of chicken, tuna, salmon and other canned meats along with packages of pasta and rice...no more last-minute trips to the grocery store.

• A roast chicken from the deli is the busy cook's secret ingredient! The chicken is already cooked and ready for whatever recipe you decide to make.

• Chicken and beef bouillon cubes are a money-saving substitute for canned broth...they save space in the pantry too. To make one cup of broth, dissolve a bouillon cube in one cup of boiling water. Use 1-3/4 cups prepared bouillon to replace a 14-ounce can of broth.

• Burgers don't have to be ordinary! Ground turkey, chicken or even ground sausage are all scrumptious. Season with seasoning blends found at the meat counter like Italian, Mexican, Southwest or Mediterranean...yum!

• Buying boneless, skinless chicken breasts in bulk? Cook them all at once. Season with salt, pepper and garlic, if desired, and allow to cool. Wrap tightly in plastic or place in a freezer bag. Kept in the freezer, they'll be ready for quick lunches, sandwiches or even zesty fajitas!

• Create a meal plan for one or even 2 weeks, including all of your favorite quick & easy meals...spaghetti on Monday, chicken pot pie on Tuesday and so forth. It can be very specific or more general. Post it on the fridge along with a shopping list...making dinner will be a snap!

• Don't forget about prepared pasta sauce in a jar when time is really short! Mix cooked chicken, pasta and veggies together in a saucepan and top it off with ready-made sauce...heat through and dinner's done.

• Just a few dinner leftovers? Keep a container in the freezer for storing these bits of meat and veggies. When the container gets full, toss everything in the slow cooker with some chicken broth or tomato juice, and you'll have a mixed-up soup at the end of the day that's never the same twice!

• Keep browned ground beef on hand for easy meal prep. Crumble several pounds of beef onto a baking pan and bake at 350 degrees until browned through, stirring often. Drain well and pack recipe portions in freezer bags.

Pot Roast & Sweet Potatoes, Page 28

# CHAPTER ONE

# Casseroles & Slow Cookers

**Chicken-Artichoke Pasta, Page 12**

**Taco-Filled Peppers, Page 26**

**Tegan Reeves,** Auburndale, FL

# Crunchy Corn Chip Chicken

Dinner in a jiffy...so quick to whip up!

*Makes 6 servings*

6 boneless, skinless chicken breasts
10-3/4 oz. can cream of chicken soup
8-oz. pkg. shredded Cheddar cheese,
    divided
1-1/4 oz. pkg. taco seasoning mix
2 c. barbecue corn chips, crushed

Arrange chicken in an ungreased 13"x9" baking pan; set aside. Combine soup, one cup cheese and taco seasoning together; spread over chicken. Bake, uncovered, at 450 degrees for 45 minutes; sprinkle with corn chips and remaining cheese. Return to oven; bake until cheese melts, about 5 minutes.

**Dianne Young,** South Jordan, UT

# Beef & Cheddar Quiche

So yummy topped with sour cream or even salsa!

*Makes 8 servings*

3 eggs, beaten
1 c. whipping cream
1 c. shredded Cheddar cheese
1 c. ground beef, browned
9-inch pie crust

Mix eggs, cream, cheese and beef together; spread into pie crust. Bake at 450 degrees for 15 minutes; lower oven temperature to 350 degrees and continue baking for 15 minutes.

★ TIME-SAVING SHORTCUT ★ Check your pantry for toppings that will dress up a casserole. Finely crushed potato chips, cheese crackers and stuffing mix add great flavor and crunch to top any casserole.

Crunchy Corn Chip Chicken

**Tamatha Knauber,** Lancaster, NY

# Beef-Spinach Biscuit Bake

Delicious...a real all-in-one meal.

### Makes 6 servings

2  7-oz. tubes refrigerated buttermilk
   biscuits
1-1/2 lbs. ground beef
1/2 c. onion, chopped
10-oz. pkg. frozen chopped spinach,
   thawed and drained
4-oz. can sliced mushrooms, drained
1 c. crumbled feta cheese or shredded
   Monterey Jack cheese
1/4 c. grated Parmesan cheese
1-1/2 t. garlic powder
salt and pepper to taste
2 T. butter, melted

Press and flatten biscuits into
the bottom and sides of a greased
11"x7" baking pan; set aside. Brown
beef and onion in a skillet over
medium heat; drain. Combine spinach
and mushrooms in a bowl; mix well.
Stir in cheeses, seasonings and beef
mixture. Spoon into prepared crust.
Drizzle with melted butter. Bake,
uncovered, at 375 degrees for 25 to
30 minutes, until bubbly and crust
is lightly golden.

★ SIMPLE INGREDIENT SWAP ★
In recipes calling for cheese, feel free to
swap out most cheeses for what you have on
hand. Mixing and matching cheese can add a
whole new flavor to tried & true recipes.

Beef-Spinach Biscuit Bake

**Sandy Rowe,** Bellevue, OH

# Pot Roast Casserole

Any type of pasta works in this recipe...even rotini!

### Makes 4 servings

**8-oz. pkg. fine egg noodles, cooked**
**2 c. beef pot roast, cooked and**
**  chopped**
**2 c. Alfredo sauce**
**1 c. sliced mushrooms**
**1/4 c. dry bread crumbs**

Mix noodles, pot roast, Alfredo sauce and mushrooms in an ungreased 2-quart casserole dish; sprinkle with bread crumbs. Bake at 350 degrees for 20 to 30 minutes, until crumbs are golden.

**Julie Davis,** Columbus, OH

# Chicken-Artichoke Pasta

Jars of Alfredo sauce and artichokes make this dish an easy and delicious weeknight favorite!

### Makes 4 servings

**16-oz. pkg. frozen grilled chicken**
**  breast strips**
**1 T. chicken bouillon granules**
**1/4 c. water**
**17-oz. jar Alfredo sauce**
**6-1/2 oz. jar marinated artichoke**
**  hearts, drained**
**6-oz. pkg. angel hair pasta, cooked**
**Optional: chopped fresh parsley**

Place chicken strips in a slow cooker with bouillon and water. Cover and cook on low setting for 2 to 3 hours. Stir in sauce and artichokes; turn slow cooker to high setting and cook an additional 30 minutes. Serve over cooked pasta; sprinkle with parsley, if desired.

Chicken-Artichoke Pasta

**Jessica Wantland,** Napoleon, OH

# Chicken Parmesan

Just six ingredients, but so yummy! Jazz it up with your favorite flavor of pasta sauce...there are lots to choose from.

### Makes 4 servings

1 egg, beaten
3/4 c. Italian-seasoned dry bread crumbs
4 boneless, skinless chicken breasts
26-oz. jar pasta sauce
1 c. shredded mozzarella cheese
cooked spaghetti

Place egg and bread crumbs in separate shallow dishes. Dip chicken into egg, then into bread crumbs. Arrange chicken in a greased 13"x9" baking pan. Bake, uncovered, at 400 degrees for 30 minutes. Spoon pasta sauce over chicken and top with cheese. Bake another 15 minutes, or until chicken juices run clear. Serve chicken and sauce over spaghetti.

**Jana Warnell,** Kalispell, MT

# Cheesy Chicken Pot Pie

I was always on the lookout for a good chicken pot pie...finally I found this one in a cookbook for kids. Now it's a family staple!

### Serves 4 to 6

2 9-inch pie crusts
2 10-3/4 oz. cans cream of potato soup
2 c. cooked chicken, cubed
15-oz. can mixed vegetables, drained
2 c. shredded Cheddar cheese

Line an ungreased 9" pie plate with one crust; set aside. Mix soup, chicken, vegetables and cheese together; spoon into pie crust. Top with remaining crust; seal and flute the edges. Cut vents in the top; bake at 350 degrees for one hour.

Chicken Parmesan

**Brenda Hager,** Nancy, KY

# Sourdough Chicken Casserole

My husband really enjoys this delicious dish, and he's not a big fan of chicken. The caramelized onions give it a great flavor!

### *Makes 4 servings*

4 c. sourdough bread, cubed
6 T. butter, melted and divided
1/3 c. grated Parmesan cheese
2 T. fresh parsley, chopped
2 sweet onions, sliced
8-oz. pkg. sliced mushrooms
10-3/4 oz. can cream of
   mushroom soup
1 c. white wine or buttermilk
2-1/2 c. cooked chicken, shredded
1/2 c. roasted red peppers,
   drained and chopped
1/2 t. salt
1/4 t. pepper

Toss together bread cubes, 1/4 cup butter, cheese and parsley in a large bowl; set aside. Sauté onions in remaining 2 tablespoons butter in a large skillet over medium-high heat 15 minutes, or until dark golden. Add mushrooms and sauté 5 minutes. Add remaining ingredients. Cook 5 more minutes, stirring constantly, until hot and bubbly. Pour into 4 lightly greased ramekins; top each ramekin with bread cube mixture. Bake, uncovered, at 400 degrees for 15 minutes, or until golden.

★ TIME-SAVING SHORTCUT ★ Caramelized onions are full of flavor and easy to make. For a big batch, add 1/2 cup butter and 6 to 8 sliced onions to a slow cooker. Cover and cook on low setting for 10 to 12 hours, stirring once or twice. Spoon onions over meat dishes or stir into casseroles to add savory flavor.

**Sourdough Chicken Casserole**

**Cherylann Smith,** Elfland, NC

# Slow-Cooker Farmhouse Pot Roast

This scrumptious roast is fall-apart tender and makes its own gravy.

### Makes 6 servings

3-lb. beef chuck roast
salt and pepper to taste
1 to 2 T. oil
8-oz. pkg. whole mushrooms
16 new redskin potatoes
1/2 lb. carrots, peeled and sliced
3 stalks celery, chopped
14-1/2 oz. can beef broth
2 c. water
23-oz. can cream of mushroom soup
Optional: chopped fresh parsley

Season roast with salt and pepper. Brown in oil on all sides in a skillet over high heat. Place roast in an ungreased slow cooker; top with vegetables. In a medium bowl, blend together broth, water and soup; pour over roast. Cover and cook on low setting 6 to 8 hours, until roast is very tender. Garnish with parsley, if desired.

**Dana Rowan,** Spokane, WA

# Cheesy Chicken & Tots Casserole

This recipe can be put together in a jiffy, as I always have the ingredients on hand. Feel free to use your own favorite cheese.

### Serves 6 to 8

32-oz. pkg. frozen potato puffs, divided
1 to 1-1/2  3-oz. pkgs. ready-to-use bacon pieces, divided
2 c. shredded sharp Cheddar cheese, divided
1 lb. boneless, skinless chicken breast, diced
garlic salt and Montreal steak seasoning or salt and pepper to taste
3/4 c. milk

To a slow cooker sprayed with non-stick vegetable spray, add half of the frozen potato puffs. Sprinkle with 1/3 each of bacon pieces and cheese. Add chicken; season as desired. Top with another 1/3 each of bacon and cheese. Arrange remaining potato puffs, bacon and cheese on top. Pour milk evenly over the top. Cover and cook on low setting for 4 to 6 hours.

**Slow-Cooker Farmhouse Pot Roast**

**Vickie,** Gooseberry Patch

# Burgundy Meatloaf

A mixture of ground beef and ground pork can also be used.

### Serves 6 to 8

2 lbs. ground beef
2 eggs, beaten
1 c. soft bread crumbs
1 onion, chopped
1/2 c. Burgundy wine or beef broth
1/2 c. fresh parsley, chopped
1 T. fresh basil, chopped
1-1/2 t. salt
1/4 t. pepper
5 slices bacon
1 bay leaf
8-oz. can tomato sauce

Combine ground beef, eggs, crumbs, onion, wine or broth, herbs and seasonings in a large bowl; mix well and set aside. Criss-cross 3 bacon slices on a 12-inch square of aluminum foil. Form beef mixture into a 6-inch round loaf on top of bacon. Cut remaining bacon slices in half; arrange on top of meatloaf. Place bay leaf on top. Lift meatloaf by aluminum foil into a slow cooker; cover and cook on high setting for one hour. Reduce heat to low setting and continue cooking, covered, for 4 more hours. Remove meatloaf from slow cooker by lifting foil. Place on a serving platter, discarding foil and bay leaf. Warm tomato sauce and spoon over sliced meatloaf.

★ FREEZE IT ★ Cut leftover meatloaf into thick slices, wrap individually and freeze, for hearty meatloaf sandwiches later on a few moments' notice.

**Burgundy Meatloaf**

**Brenda Bodnar,** Mayfield Village, OH

# Sweet & Spicy Roast Beef

I've been making this for years...the heavenly smell of the slow-simmering beef warms heart & soul and piques the appetite.

### Serves 8 to 10

1 onion, sliced and separated
   into rings
3 to 4-lb. bottom-round beef roast
1 T. garlic powder
1 t. pepper
12-oz. can regular or non-alcoholic
   beer
1 c. catsup
1/4 c. brown sugar, packed
3 T. all-purpose flour
1 T. prepared horseradish, or to taste

Add onion rings to a lightly greased slow cooker; set aside. Sprinkle roast on all sides with garlic powder and pepper; add to slow cooker. Combine remaining ingredients in a bowl; mix well and spoon over roast. Cover and cook on low setting for 8 to 10 hours. Remove roast from slow cooker and slice; serve topped with sauce from slow cooker.

**Theresa Beach,** Lexington, SC

# Saucy Mozzarella Chicken

A real family-pleaser...we serve it over angel hair pasta.

### Makes 6 servings

6 boneless, skinless chicken breasts
salt and pepper to taste
26-oz. jar spaghetti sauce
8-oz. pkg. shredded mozzarella
   cheese

Season chicken with salt and pepper; arrange in an ungreased 13"x9" baking pan. Pour spaghetti sauce on top; bake at 350 degrees for one hour and 10 minutes. Sprinkle with cheese; return to oven until melted, an additional 5 to 10 minutes.

Sweet & Spicy Roast Beef

**Mariann Raftery,** Scarsdale, NY

# Hot Cherry Pepper Chicken

Long and slow is the way to go with this flavorful dish! For adults I use the whole jar of peppers, because they love the hot spicy taste. I use fewer peppers when cooking for children.

### *Serves 6 to 8*

1 T. olive oil
1 onion, sliced
4 to 6 cloves garlic, chopped
salt and pepper to taste
12 chicken drumsticks, thighs
   and wings
32-oz. jar hot cherry peppers, divided
1/4 t. salt
pepper to taste

In an ungreased deep 13"x9" baking pan, combine oil, onion, garlic, salt and pepper; stir to mix. Add chicken; toss together well. Pour 1/2 jar of cherry peppers with juice over chicken. Bake, uncovered, at 325 degrees for 45 minutes; turn chicken over. If desired, for a very spicy dish, pour remaining peppers and juice over chicken. Cook, uncovered, another 60 minutes, or until chicken juices run clear, turning chicken over several times.

★ SIMPLE INGREDIENT SWAP ★ **Not a fan of spicy food? Substitute about 1-1/2 cups sliced red bell pepper for the hot cherry peppers in this recipe. You'll get the same bright red color and great flavor, but none of the heat.**

Hot Cherry Pepper Chicken

**Shannon Reents,** Belleville, OH

# Taco-Filled Peppers

My family loves stuffed peppers and Mexican food, so I came up with this two-in-one dish for them.

*Makes 4 servings*

1 lb. ground beef
1-oz. pkg. taco seasoning mix
1 c. salsa
15-1/2 oz. can kidney beans, drained
4 green peppers, tops removed
1 tomato, chopped
1/2 c. shredded Cheddar cheese
1/2 c. sour cream

Brown beef in a skillet over medium heat; drain. Stir in seasoning mix, salsa and beans; bring to a boil. Simmer for 5 minutes. Meanwhile, add peppers to a large saucepan of boiling water. Cook for 3 to 5 minutes; rinse peppers in cold water and drain well. Spoon 1/2 cup beef mixture into each pepper; arrange peppers in an ungreased 9"x9" baking pan. Cover and bake at 350 degrees for 10 to 12 minutes, or until hot and bubbly. Top with tomato and cheese; serve with sour cream.

**Tamara Fennell,** FPO, AE

# Hawaiian Chicken

For an extra-yummy treat, add a thin slice of grilled ham and top with provolone cheese before baking.

*Makes 8 servings*

3 c. pineapple chunks with juice
1 c. soy sauce
1 t. ground ginger
1/4 t. garlic, chopped
4 lbs. chicken breasts

Mix all ingredients except chicken together. Add chicken; marinate for 4 hours in the refrigerator. Grill chicken until browned; arrange in an ungreased 13"x9" baking pan. Bake, uncovered, at 325 degrees for one hour.

★ PENNY PINCHER ★ Try using a little less ground beef in tried & true recipes like Taco-Filled Peppers. Add a few more veggies like corn, peas or green beans...chances are good that no one will even notice!

Taco-Filled Peppers

Barbara Schmeckpeper, Minoka, IL

# Pot Roast & Sweet Potatoes

The sweet potatoes have such a good flavor in this recipe.

### Serves 4 to 6

2 T. oil

1-1/2 to 2-lb. boneless beef chuck roast

1 onion, thinly sliced

3 sweet potatoes, peeled and quartered

2/3 c. beef broth

3/4 t. celery salt

1/4 t. salt

1/4 t. pepper

1/4 t. cinnamon

1 T. cornstarch

2 T. cold water

Heat oil in a skillet over medium heat. Add roast and brown on all sides; drain. Place onion and sweet potatoes in a 4-quart slow cooker; top with roast. Combine beef broth and seasonings; pour over roast. Cover and cook on low setting for 7 to 8 hours, or on high setting 4 to 5 hours. Place roast on a serving platter; surround with vegetables and keep warm. Combine cornstarch and water in a small saucepan; add one cup of juices from slow cooker. Cook and stir over medium heat until thickened and bubbly; continue cooking and stirring 2 more minutes. Serve gravy with roast.

★ DOUBLE DUTY ★ Slow-cooked beef chuck roast is always a winner! Any leftovers will be equally delicious in sandwiches, soups or casseroles, so be sure to choose the largest size roast your slow cooker will hold.

**Pot Roast & Sweet Potatoes**

**Betty Lou Wright,** Hendersonville, TN

# Top-Prize Chicken Casserole

This crowd-pleasing dish has graced my family's table for decades. Originally prepared by my mother-in-law, it's been taken to many potlucks and church suppers. With its creamy sauce and crunchy topping, it's always a hit.

### Serves 6 to 8

2 to 3 c. cooked chicken, cubed
2  10-3/4 oz. cans cream of
   mushroom soup
4 eggs, hard-boiled, peeled and
   chopped
1 onion, chopped
2 c. cooked rice
1-1/2 c. celery, chopped
1 c. mayonnaise
2 T. lemon juice
3-oz. pkg. slivered almonds
5-oz. can chow mein noodles

Combine all ingredients except almonds and noodles in a large bowl; mix well. Transfer mixture to a lightly greased 3-quart casserole dish. Cover and refrigerate 8 hours to overnight. Stir in almonds. Bake, uncovered, at 350 degrees for 40 to 45 minutes, until heated through. Top with noodles; bake 5 more minutes.

**Betty Richer,** Grand Junction, CO

# Russian Chicken

Not the same old chicken... everyone will ask what's in it!

### Makes 4 servings

3 to 4 lbs. chicken
1/4 c. mayonnaise
1-1/2 oz. pkg. onion soup mix
1/2 c. Russian salad dressing
1 c. apricot-pineapple preserves

Arrange chicken in an ungreased 13"x9" baking pan; set aside. Mix remaining ingredients; spread over chicken. Bake at 350 degrees for 1-1/4 hours, or until chicken juices run clear when pierced.

**Top-Prize Chicken Casserole**

Jean Carter, Rockledge, FL

# Swiss Steak

I have served this for years to a variety of very picky eaters...they all loved it! Serve with buttery mashed potatoes.

### Serves 4 to 6

2-lb. boneless beef round steak, cut
    into 4 to 6 serving-size pieces
1.1-oz. pkg. beefy onion soup mix
3 c. onion, sliced
28-oz. can diced tomatoes
3 T. all-purpose flour
1 c. water
Garnish: minced fresh parsley

Arrange steak in a slow cooker. Sprinkle soup mix over steak; arrange onion slices all around. Top with undrained tomatoes. Cover and cook on low setting for 8 hours, or on high setting for 4 hours. Remove steak and vegetables to a serving dish; set aside. Mix together flour and water in a small bowl; add to juices in slow cooker and stir until thickened. Spoon gravy over steak to serve. Sprinkle with parsley.

★ SIMPLE INGREDIENT SWAP ★
A delicious secret the next time you make mashed potatoes...substitute equal parts chicken broth and cream for the milk in any favorite mashed potato recipe.

**Swiss Steak**

**Jennifer Holmes,** Philadelphia, PA

# Fruity Baked Chicken

Serve over steamed rice with a side of asparagus spears...delicious!

*Makes 6 servings*

2 T. olive oil
6 boneless, skinless chicken breasts
3 lemons, halved
3 oranges, halved
1 apple, peeled, cored and chopped

Coat the bottom of a 13"x9" baking pan with olive oil; arrange chicken breasts in pan. Squeeze juice from one lemon and one orange over chicken; set aside. Slice remaining lemons and oranges into wedges; cut these in half. Arrange around and on top of chicken breasts; add apple. Cover and bake at 375 degrees for one hour and 45 minutes; uncover for last 30 minutes of baking

**Paulette Alexander,**
Newfoundland, Canada

# Cream Cheese-Stuffed Chicken

One of our favorite meals! It's so easy to make and leaves everybody quite satisfied. I sometimes make it when cooking as a volunteer with elementary children at our local school.

*Makes 4 servings*

4 boneless, skinless chicken breasts
1/2 c. cream cheese with chives, softened
4 T. butter, softened and divided
1/2 c. brown sugar, packed
1/4 c. mustard
4 wooden toothpicks, soaked in water
Optional: cooked rice

Place each chicken breast between 2 pieces of plastic wrap. Pound to 1/4-inch thick and set aside. In a small bowl, beat cream cheese and 2 tablespoons butter to a creamy consistency. Blend in brown sugar and mustard. Divide mixture among chicken breasts; spread evenly. Fold chicken over; fasten with toothpicks. Place chicken in a single layer in a lightly greased 9"x9" baking pan. Melt remaining butter and drizzle over chicken. Bake, uncovered, at 350 degrees for 25 to 30 minutes, until chicken juices run clear. Discard toothpicks. Serve with cooked rice, if desired.

Fruity Baked Chicken

**Britni Rexwinkle,** Green Forest, AR

# Upside-Down Mexican Pot Pie

This is the first recipe my husband and I came up with together in college...we just tossed together some things we had on hand. It was a keeper! Sometimes I substitute shredded chicken.

### Makes 6 servings

1 lb. ground beef
1 onion, chopped
1 green pepper, chopped
1 zucchini, chopped
4-oz. can diced green chiles
14-1/2 oz. can diced tomatoes
11-oz. can corn, drained
8-1/2 oz. pkg. cornbread mix
1 c. shredded Mexican-blend cheese

In a skillet over medium-high heat, brown beef with onion, green pepper, zucchini and chiles; drain. Add tomatoes with juice and corn; simmer for about 5 minutes. Meanwhile, prepare cornbread mix according to package directions; pour batter into a lightly greased 2-quart casserole dish. Spoon beef mixture over batter; sprinkle with cheese. Bake, covered with aluminum foil, at 350 degrees for 25 minutes. Uncover; bake an additional 5 minutes, or until cheese is melted.

★ SPICY SECRET ★ Cilantro, otherwise known as "Mexican parsley," has a hot, spicy, minty flavor. Sprinkle fresh leaves on spicy Mexican and Indian dishes.

Cheeseburger & Fries Casserole

**Regina Vining,** Warwick, RI

# Cornbread-Topped Beef Bake

Use a cast-iron skillet...just pop it right into the oven for one-pot convenience!

### Makes 6 servings

3 slices bacon
1/2 lb. ground beef
1 onion, chopped
10-3/4 oz. can tomato soup
2/3 c. water
2  16-oz. cans black beans, drained
   and rinsed
1 t. chili powder
1/2 t. garlic powder
Optional: 1/4 t. red pepper flakes
1 c. shredded Cheddar cheese
8-1/2 oz. pkg. cornbread mix
Garnish: shredded Cheddar cheese

In a skillet over medium heat, cook bacon until crisp. Set aside bacon, reserving drippings in skillet. Brown beef and onion in reserved drippings; drain. Stir in soup, water, crumbled bacon, beans and seasonings. Simmer over low heat for 20 minutes, stirring often and adding a little more water, if needed. Sprinkle cheese over beef mixture; mix well. Transfer to a lightly greased 13"x9" baking pan; set aside. Prepare cornbread mix according to package directions; spread batter over beef mixture. Bake, uncovered, at 400 degrees for 20 to 30 minutes, until bubbly and cornbread is golden. Top with additional cheese.

★ TIME-SAVING SHORTCUT ★ Get out Grandma's cast-iron skillet for the tastiest stovetop meals. Cast iron provides even heat distribution for speedy cooking and crisp golden crusts. It can even be popped directly into the oven or under a broiler to finish cooking.

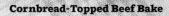

**Cornbread-Topped Beef Bake**

**Jennifer Levy,** Warners, NY

# Slow-Cooker Rich Beef Stew

This recipe was given to me by my sister Karen. We both make it often for family meals, and we're proud to serve it to company too! It's delicious... even our picky kids eat it and ask for seconds. Serve with crusty bread to enjoy all the scrumptious gravy.

### Makes 6 servings

2-1/2 lbs. stew beef cubes
10-3/4 oz. can cream of mushroom
  soup
10-3/4 oz. can French onion soup
1 c. dry red wine or beef broth
1 c. sliced mushrooms
cooked egg noodles

Combine all ingredients except noodles in a slow cooker; stir to mix. Cover and cook on low setting for 8 to 10 hours. Serve over cooked noodles.

**Pat Habiger,** Spearville, KS

# Steak & Rice Casserole

A hearty casserole recipe you can count on.

### Serves 6 to 8

2 green peppers, finely chopped
2 celery stalks, finely chopped
4 carrots, peeled and sliced
2 lbs. beef round steak, cut in strips
1/2 c. milk
10-3/4 oz. can cream of celery soup
10-3/4 oz. can cream of onion soup
1-1/2 c. cooked rice

Arrange peppers, celery, carrots and steak in a slow cooker. Mix milk and soups; pour over top. Cover and cook on low setting for 6 hours. Add rice; cover and cook on high setting for one hour. Add additional water or milk if liquid is absorbed.

★ PENNY PINCHER ★ Slow cooking works wonders on inexpensive, less-tender cuts of beef... arm and chuck roast, rump roast, short ribs, round steak and stew beef cook up juicy and delicious.

**Slow-Cooker Rich Beef Stew**

Amy James, Fayetteville, AR

# Fantastic 40-Clove Chicken

You'll be amazed at how sweet and flavorful the garlic is after cooking all day. You can usually buy already-peeled garlic in the produce section.

*Serves 6 to 8*

4 boneless, skinless chicken breasts
2 t. salt
1 t. pepper
40 cloves garlic, peeled
3/4 c. dry white wine or chicken
    broth
1 t. dried thyme
1-1/2 t. dried rosemary
1 bay leaf
1 T. butter

Season chicken with salt and pepper; place in a slow cooker. Add garlic, wine or broth and seasonings to slow cooker. Cover and cook on low setting for 4 to 6 hours, until chicken juices run clear. Remove chicken from slow cooker and pour juices through a strainer, mashing some garlic cloves through as well. Discard bay leaf. Cook juice mixture in a saucepan over high heat until thickened, about 6 to 8 minutes. Add butter to sauce; stir until mixed. Drizzle sauce over chicken.

★ STORE IT ★ Store onions and garlic away from other produce, in a dark well-ventilated pantry...they can cause other vegetables to soften when stored together.

Fantastic 40-Clove Chicken

**Sandra Sullivan,** Aurora, CT

# Chicken with Artichokes & Capers

Quick, easy and a hit with the whole family! Add a simple side salad and warm bread...you'll have a gourmet dinner in no time.

### Serves 6 to 8

3 lbs. boneless, skinless chicken
   thighs
salt and pepper to taste
14-1/2 oz. can diced tomatoes
14-oz. can artichoke hearts, drained
1/4 c. capers
2 to 3 cloves garlic, thinly sliced
3 tomatoes, chopped
8-oz. pkg. sliced mushrooms
16-oz. pkg. spaghetti, cooked

Season chicken with salt and pepper; place in a slow cooker. Spoon canned tomatoes with juice, artichokes, capers and garlic over chicken. Cover and cook on high setting for 3 to 4 hours, until chicken juices run clear. Stir in fresh tomatoes and mushrooms during the last 30 minutes of cooking. Serve chicken and sauce over spaghetti.

**Stephanie Mayer,** Portsmouth, VA

# Slowly Deviled Beef

This cooks all day, but is worth the wait!

### Makes 4 servings

2 lbs. stew beef cubes
1.4-oz. pkg. Sloppy Joe seasoning mix
1 c. celery, sliced
1 green pepper, chopped
1/2 c. water
2 T. vinegar
cooked rice or egg noodles

Combine all ingredients except rice or noodles in a slow cooker; stir to mix. Cover and cook on low setting for 8 to 10 hours, or on high setting for 4-1/2 to 5 hours. Serve over cooked rice or noodles.

Chicken with Artichokes & Capers

**Dorothy Benson,** Baton Rouge, LA

# Chicken Spaghetti Deluxe

This recipe is reminiscent of cold winter days and the inviting smells of Mom's warm kitchen. Best of all, the pasta doesn't need to be cooked ahead of time.

### *Makes 8 servings*

2 c. cooked chicken, chopped

8-oz. pkg. spaghetti, uncooked and broken into 2-inch pieces

1 c. celery, chopped

1 c. onion, chopped

1 c. yellow pepper, chopped

1 c. red pepper, chopped

2  10-3/4 oz. cans cream of mushroom soup

1 c. chicken broth

1/4 t. Cajun seasoning or pepper

1 c. shredded Cheddar cheese

Mix chicken, spaghetti, celery, onion, yellow pepper and red pepper in a bowl. Whisk together soup, broth and seasoning in a separate bowl. Add chicken mixture to soup mixture. Spread chicken mixture in a lightly greased 13"x9" baking pan; sprinkle cheese over top. Cover with aluminum foil coated with non-stick vegetable spray. Bake at 350 degrees for 45 minutes. Uncover and bake for 10 more minutes.

★ HOT TIP ★ Char bell peppers to give them a delicious sweet, smoky taste. Arrange peppers on an aluminum foil-lined broiler pan. Broil for 20 to 25 minutes, until peppers are blackened and soft, turning them with tongs every five minutes. Cool. The skins will remove easily; discard the seeds also.

Chicken Spaghetti Deluxe

**Vicki Cox,** Bland, MO

# Beefy Chow Mein Noodle Casserole

This tastes great with ground chicken or turkey, too!

### Makes 16 servings

2 lbs. ground beef
1 onion, chopped
10-3/4 oz. can cream of celery soup
10-3/4 oz. can golden mushroom soup
1-1/4 c. water
1 c. instant rice, uncooked
1 T. Worcestershire sauce
1 t. garlic powder
1/2 t. salt
5-oz. can chow mein noodles
Garnish: chopped fresh parsley

Brown ground beef and onion in a large skillet over medium heat; drain. Stir together soups and remaining ingredients except noodles and garnish in a large bowl. Add to beef mixture; mix well. Pour into a lightly greased 13"x9" baking pan. Bake, uncovered, at 375 degrees for 20 minutes, or until bubbly. Sprinkle with chow mein noodles. Bake, uncovered, an additional 5 to 10 minutes. Garnish with parsley.

**Tami Hoffman,** Litchfield, NH

# Creamy Apricot Chicken

Serve over a bed of white rice.

### Serves 4 to 6

8-oz. jar Russian salad dressing
12-oz. jar apricot preserves
1 to 2 lbs. boneless, skinless chicken breasts

Combine salad dressing and preserves together; set aside. Arrange chicken in a slow cooker; pour dressing mixture on top. Heat on low setting for 6 to 8 hours.

★ SIMPLE INGREDIENT SWAP ★
Crisp salads are super with casserole dinners. Shake up the "usual" salad by mixing in some raisins, toffee-glazed almonds, crumbled feta or blue cheese, chow mein noodles or halved grapes...a tasty change of pace.

**Beefy Chow Mein Noodle Casserole**

**Joan Brochu,** Hardwick, VT

# Braciola Stuffed Beef

If you've never tried this, you don't know what you're missing!

### *Makes 6 servings*

2 lbs. boneless beef round steak
1/2 c. seasoned dry bread crumbs
1/2 c. grated Parmesan cheese
1 T. garlic, minced
1 egg, beaten
1/4 t. pepper
2 eggs, hard-boiled, peeled and
   minced
32-oz. jar meatless spaghetti sauce,
   divided
hot cooked linguine pasta

Place steak between 2 lengths of wax paper; pound until thin and set aside. Mix together bread crumbs, cheese, garlic, egg, pepper and minced eggs in a bowl; spread over steak. Roll up steak and tie at one-inch intervals with kitchen string. Spread one cup spaghetti sauce in the bottom of a slow cooker; set a rack on top. Place rolled-up steak on rack; cover with remaining sauce. Cover and cook on low setting for 6 to 8 hours, until steak is very tender. Slice between strings and serve over hot linguine.

---

★ SIMPLE INGREDIENT SWAP ★
**For a flavorful change, substitute crushed herb-flavored stuffing mix for dry bread crumbs in any casserole.**

---

**Braciola Stuffed Beef**

**Brenda Flowers,** Olney, IL

# Easy Gumbo Meatballs

After baking, keep these warm in the slow cooker...they're a potluck favorite!

*Makes 6 servings*

2 lbs. ground beef
4 slices bread, crumbled
3/4 c. evaporated milk
10-3/4 oz. can chicken gumbo soup
10-1/2 oz. can French onion soup

Combine first 3 ingredients; form into one-inch balls. Arrange in an ungreased 13"x9" baking pan; pour soups on top. Bake at 350 degrees for 1-1/2 hours.

**Cheri Emery,** Quincy, IL

# Cheddar Barbecue

A hearty meal the whole family will enjoy.

*Makes 6 servings*

1-1/2 lb. ground beef
1 c. onion, chopped
16-oz. can barbecue-style beans
10-3/4 oz. can tomato soup
1 t. chili powder
1/2 t. salt
1/2 t. paprika
1/4 t. garlic salt
12-oz. tube refrigerated biscuits
1 c. shredded Cheddar cheese

Brown ground beef and onion together; drain. Add beans, soup and seasonings; bring to a boil. Spread mixture into a greased 2-quart casserole dish. Arrange biscuits on top of mixture; sprinkle with cheese. Bake at 375 degrees for 25 to 30 minutes.

★ HOT TIP ★ Serve a hearty dish like Easy Gumbo Meatballs over rice or noodles, or even as a tasty appetizer on game day!

**Easy Gumbo Meatballs**

**Michelle Greeley,** Hayes, VA

# Gourmet Beef-Noodle Casserole

Cream cheese and Cheddar cheese make this casserole extra rich and creamy.

*Serves 6 to 8*

1 lb. ground beef
14-1/2 oz. can diced tomatoes
8-oz. can tomato sauce
1/2 c. green pepper, chopped
4-oz. can sliced mushrooms, drained
1 clove garlic, chopped
2 t. salt
2 t. sugar
1/2 c. Burgundy wine or beef broth
8-oz. pkg. cream cheese, softened
1 c. sour cream
1/3 c. onion, chopped
2 c. shredded Cheddar cheese, divided
8-oz. pkg. wide egg noodles, cooked
   and divided

Brown ground beef in a skillet over medium-high heat; drain. Add tomatoes with juice, sauce, green pepper, mushrooms, garlic, salt, sugar and wine or broth; cover and simmer over low heat 10 minutes. In a medium bowl, blend cream cheese, sour cream, onion and one cup Cheddar cheese; set aside. In an ungreased 13"x9" baking pan, layer half the beef mixture, half the noodles and half the cream cheese mixture; repeat layers. Top with remaining Cheddar cheese. Bake, uncovered, at 350 degrees for 40 minutes.

★ SIMPLE INGREDIENT SWAP ★
**For a healthy change, give whole-wheat noodles a try in your favorite casserole... they taste great and contain more fiber than regular noodles.**

**Gourmet Beef-Noodle Casserole**

**Julie Whiteside,** Queenstown, MD

# Hamburger Bundles

Make your cooking time even less by preparing the stuffing mix according to the microwave directions.

### Makes 4 servings

10-3/4 oz. can cream of mushroom soup
1/4 c. milk
1 lb. ground beef
1 T. catsup
2 t. Worcestershire sauce
6-oz. pkg. stuffing mix, cooked

In a medium bowl, blend together soup and milk. In a large bowl, combine beef, catsup and Worcestershire sauce. Divide mixture and shape into 4 patties. Place 1/4 cup of stuffing onto each patty and draw sides up to make a ball. Place in an ungreased 13"x9" baking pan; cover with soup mixture. Bake, uncovered, at 350 degrees for 35 to 45 minutes.

**Lauren Williams,** Kewanee, MO

# Easy Enchilada Casserole

We love this casserole...it combines so many textures and flavors! Top it with sour cream and salsa for a southwestern-style feast.

### Makes 8 servings

2 lbs. ground beef
1 onion, chopped
10-oz. can enchilada sauce
10-3/4 oz. can cream of mushroom soup
10-3/4 oz. can cream of chicken soup
16-oz. pkg. shredded Cheddar cheese
6-oz. pkg. corn chips

In a large skillet over medium heat, brown beef and onion; drain well. Stir in sauce and soups. Transfer beef mixture to a lightly greased 13"x9" baking pan; top with cheese and corn chips. Bake, uncovered, at 350 degrees for 45 minutes, or until hot and bubbly.

Hamburger Bundles

**Carol Wingo,** Henderson, TX

# Tomato-Beef Noodle Bake

Add a few diced mushrooms when you're browning the beef for extra flavor.

### Makes 4 servings

1 lb. ground beef
1 onion, chopped
10-oz. can diced tomatoes with green chiles
10-3/4 oz. can cream of mushroom soup
8-oz. pkg. fine egg noodles, cooked

Brown beef and onion in a skillet over medium heat; drain. Add remaining ingredients; place in an ungreased 2-quart casserole dish. Bake at 350 degrees for 20 to 25 minutes, until hot and bubbly.

**Maggie Dow,** North Royalton, OH

# Sloppy Joe Bake

Sloppy Joes you can eat with a knife & fork...all of the flavor, but less mess!

### Makes 8 servings

1-1/2 lbs. ground beef
1/4 c. onion, chopped
1/4 c. green pepper, chopped
15-1/2 oz. can Sloppy Joe sauce
8-oz. pkg. shredded Cheddar cheese
2 c. biscuit baking mix
2 eggs, beaten
1 c. milk

In a skillet over medium heat, brown beef, onion and green pepper; drain. Stir in sauce. Spoon mixture into a greased 13"x9" baking pan; sprinkle with cheese. In a bowl, stir together remaining ingredients just until blended. Spoon over cheese. Bake, uncovered, at 400 degrees for about 25 minutes, until golden. Cut into squares.

Sloppy Joe Bake

**Stephanie Westfall,** Dallas, GA

# Perfect Pepper Steak

This recipe is one of my family's favorites! Sprinkle with chow mein noodles if you like a crunchy topping.

### Serves 4 to 6

1-1/2 to 2 lbs. beef round steak, sliced
   into strips
15-oz. can diced tomatoes
1 to 2 green and/or red peppers, sliced
1 onion, chopped
4-oz. can sliced mushrooms, drained
1/4 c. salsa
cooked rice

Combine all ingredients except rice in a slow cooker. Cover and cook on low setting for 6 to 8 hours. To serve, spoon over cooked rice.

**Vicki Lanzendorf,** Madison, WI

# Chuck Wagon Mac

One of my favorites when I was a kid, and it still is to this day. Any leftovers are tasty too...although with a 17-year-old son who's well over 6 feet tall, leftovers are rare!

### Makes 6 servings

7-1/4 oz. pkg. macaroni & cheese mix
1 lb. ground beef
1/2 c. celery, sliced
1/2 c. onion, diced
2 c. frozen corn, thawed
6-oz. can tomato paste
salt and pepper to taste

Prepare macaroni & cheese mix as package directs. Meanwhile, brown beef in a skillet over medium heat; drain. Add celery and onion to beef; cook until tender. Stir in corn, tomato paste, salt and pepper; mix with prepared macaroni & cheese. Spoon into a greased 2-quart casserole dish. Bake, uncovered, at 350 degrees for 20 minutes, or until heated through.

**Perfect Pepper Steak**

Italian Meatball Soup, Page 116

# CHAPTER TWO

# Soups & Salads

**Raspberry & Chicken Salad, Page 82**　　**Chicken-Tortellini Soup, Page 80**

**Becky Butler,** Keller, TX

# Apple-Walnut Chicken Salad

This tasty recipe uses the convenience of a roast chicken from your grocery store's deli. What a great time-saver!

### *Makes 6 servings*

6 c. mixed field greens or baby greens
2 c. deli roast chicken, boned and
    shredded
1/3 c. crumbled blue cheese
1/4 c. chopped walnuts, toasted
1 Fuji or Gala apple, cored and
    sliced

In a large salad bowl, toss together all ingredients. Drizzle Balsamic Apple Vinaigrette over salad, tossing gently to coat. Serve immediately.

### *Balsamic Apple Vinaigrette:*

2 T. frozen apple juice
    concentrate
1 T. cider vinegar
1 T. white balsamic vinegar
1 t. Dijon mustard
1/4 t. garlic powder
1/3 c. olive oil

Whisk together all ingredients in a small bowl.

**Christian Brown,** Killeen, TX

# Chicken Broth From Scratch

Everyone needs a good recipe for homemade chicken broth! Use the broth right away in a recipe or freeze for later use.

### *Makes 8 cups*

3 to 4-lb. roasting chicken
2 carrots, peeled and thickly sliced
2 stalks celery, thickly sliced
1 onion, halved
1 clove garlic, halved
2 T. olive oil
2 qts. cold water
4 sprigs fresh parsley
4 sprigs fresh thyme
2 bay leaves
**Optional: salt and pepper to taste**

Place chicken in an ungreased roasting pan. Cover and roast at 350 degrees for 1-1/2 hours, or until juices run clear when chicken is pierced with a fork. Cool chicken and shred. Reserve pan drippings and bones. Use shredded chicken in your favorite recipe or freeze for later use. Sauté vegetables and garlic in oil in a stockpot over medium heat for 3 minutes. Add reserved bones, pan drippings, water and seasonings; simmer for one hour. Strain broth; season with salt and pepper, if desired.

**Apple-Walnut Chicken Salad**

**Francie Stutzman,** Dalton, OH

# Chicken & Rice Salad

This dish is scrumptious...I hope you'll try it!

***Makes 4 servings***

3 T. red wine vinegar
1-1/2 T. extra-virgin olive oil
1/4 t. pepper
1 clove garlic, minced
2 c. long-grain rice, cooked
1-1/2 c. cooked chicken breast, diced
1/2 c. jarred roasted red peppers,
    drained and diced
1/2 c. Kalamata olives, halved
    and pitted
1/4 c. fresh chives, chopped
1/4 c. fresh basil, chopped
1/4 c. fresh oregano, chopped
14-oz. can artichokes, drained
    and diced
4-oz. pkg. crumbled feta cheese

In a small bowl, whisk together vinegar, olive oil, pepper and garlic; set aside. In a separate bowl, combine rice and remaining ingredients except cheese. At serving time, drizzle vinegar mixture over salad; sprinkle with cheese.

★ SIMPLE INGREDIENT SWAP ★
There are many imported olives you can try in pastas and salads...huge purple Alfonsos, sharp and spicy Sicilians, flavorful Ligurias from Italy; rich Kalamatas and Royals from Greece; tender, savory Nicoise and crisp Picholines from France. Ask to try a variety of olives at your local gourmet deli.

Chicken & Rice Salad

**Erin McRae,** Beaverton, OR

# Slow-Cooker Beefy Taco Soup

Top each bowl of this hearty soup with feta cheese and serve with taco chips. Yum!

### Serves 4 to 6

1 lb. ground beef, browned
15-oz. can stewed tomatoes
15-oz. can kidney beans, drained and rinsed
1-1/4 oz. pkg. taco seasoning mix
8-oz. can tomato sauce
Optional: feta cheese

Stir together all ingredients; pour into a 3 to 4-quart slow cooker. Cover and cook on low setting for 6 to 8 hours; stir occasionally.

**Olivia Gust,** Woodburn, OR

# Chicken & Wild Rice Soup

This soup is great on a cold winter's day, served with homemade bread right out of the oven.

### Makes 6 servings

6 c. water
6-oz. pkg. long-grain and wild rice mix
2-oz. pkg. chicken noodle soup mix
2 stalks celery, sliced
1 carrot, peeled and chopped
1/2 c. onion, chopped
2  10-3/4 oz. cans cream of chicken soup
2 c. cooked chicken, chopped
salt and pepper to taste

Bring water to a boil in a large stockpot over medium-high heat. Stir in rice mix with seasoning packet and noodle soup mix. Bring to a boil. Cover and simmer over medium-low heat for 10 minutes, stirring occasionally. Add celery, carrot and onion. Cover and simmer 10 minutes, stirring occasionally. Mix in soup, chicken, salt and pepper. Cover and simmer 10 minutes more, stirring occasionally, until rice and vegetables are tender.

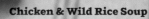
**Chicken & Wild Rice Soup**

**Renae Scheiderer,** Beallsville, OH

# Chicken & Barley Chili

I found this recipe and adjusted it a bit to our family's taste. I'm happy to report that it's a hit!

### Serves 8 to 10

14-1/2 oz. can diced tomatoes
16-oz. jar salsa
14-1/2 oz. can chicken broth
1 c. pearled barley, uncooked
3 c. water
1 T. chili powder
1 t. ground cumin
15-oz. can kidney beans, drained
   and rinsed
15-1/4 oz. can corn, drained
3 c. cooked chicken breast, cut into
   bite-size pieces
Optional: shredded Cheddar cheese,
   sour cream

In a stockpot, combine undrained tomatoes, salsa, chicken broth, barley, water and seasonings. Bring to a boil over high heat. Cover and reduce heat to low; simmer for 20 minutes, stirring occasionally. Add beans, corn and chicken. Increase heat to high; bring to a boil. Cover and reduce heat to low. Simmer for another 5 minutes, or until barley is tender. Ladle into bowls. Top with cheese and sour cream, if desired.

★ HOT TIP ★ To mellow out the sharp taste that tomatoes can have, stir a teaspoonful of sugar into a simmering pot of chili, tomato soup or spaghetti sauce.

Chicken & Barley Chili

**Lisa Seckora,** Bloomer, WI

# Pasta Taco Salad

Great at potlucks and family gatherings...everyone loves this salad with a kick!

### Serves 12 to 14

3 c. rotini pasta, uncooked
1 lb. ground beef
1-1/4 oz. pkg. taco seasoning mix
3/4 c. water
7 c. lettuce, torn
2 tomatoes, chopped
8-oz. pkg. shredded Cheddar cheese
2 c. nacho-flavored tortilla chips, crushed

Cook pasta according to package directions; drain and rinse with cold water. Meanwhile, brown beef in a skillet over medium heat; drain. Add taco seasoning and water; cook and stir until thickened. In a large bowl, combine pasta, beef and Dressing; toss until coated. Add lettuce, tomatoes and cheese; toss to combine. Sprinkle with tortilla chips.

### Dressing:

1-1/4 c. mayonnaise
3 T. milk
3-3/4 t. sugar
3-3/4 t. cider vinegar
1 T. dry mustard

Whisk together all ingredients.

★ SIMPLE INGREDIENT SWAP ★
Try using a different shape of pasta next time you make Pasta Taco Salad. Wagon wheels, seashells and bow ties all hold dressing well...they're fun for kids too!

Pasta Taco Salad

**Judy Phelan,** Macomb, IL

# Hearty Hamburger Stew

A comforting weeknight meal... and with just one pan, clean-up will be a breeze!

### Makes 4 servings

1 lb. lean ground beef
1 onion, chopped
1/2 c. celery, chopped
5-1/2 c. no-salt tomato juice
1 c. water
1/2 c. pearled barley, uncooked
2 t. chili powder
salt and pepper to taste

In a large saucepan over medium heat, cook beef, onion and celery until beef is no longer pink. Drain; stir in remaining ingredients. Bring to a boil; reduce heat to low. Cover and simmer, stirring occasionally, for 50 minutes, or until barley is tender.

**Heather Quinn,** Gilmer, TX

# Tomato-Ravioli Soup

This soup has a light, smooth flavor...there's always an empty pot afterwards!

### Serves 6 to 8

1 lb. ground beef
28-oz. can crushed tomatoes
6-oz. can tomato paste
2 c. water
1-1/2 c. onion, chopped
2 cloves garlic, minced
1/4 c. fresh parsley, chopped
3/4 t. dried basil
1/2 t. dried oregano
1/4 t. dried thyme
1/2 t. onion salt
1/2 t. salt
1/4 t. pepper
1/2 t. sugar
9-oz. pkg. frozen cheese ravioli, uncooked
1/4 c. grated Parmesan cheese

In a Dutch oven, cook beef over medium heat until no longer pink; drain. Stir in tomatoes with juice, tomato paste, water, onion, garlic, seasonings and sugar. Bring to a boil. Reduce heat; cover and simmer for 30 minutes. Meanwhile, cook ravioli as package directs; drain. Add ravioli to soup and heat through. Stir in Parmesan cheese; serve immediately.

Hearty Hamburger Stew

**Evelyn Belcher,** Monroeton, PA

# Grandma's Chicken Noodle Soup

My daughter gave me this recipe years ago...now it's my favorite!

*Makes 8 servings*

16-oz. pkg. thin egg noodles,
   uncooked
1 t. oil
12 c. chicken broth
1-1/2 t. salt
1 t. poultry seasoning
1 c. celery, chopped
1 c. onion, chopped
Optional: 1 c. carrot, peeled
   and chopped
1/3 c. cornstarch
1/4 c. cold water
4 c. cooked chicken, diced

Cook noodles according to package directions; drain, toss with oil and set aside. In the same pot, combine chicken broth and seasonings; bring to a boil over medium heat. Stir in vegetables; reduce heat to medium-low. Cover and simmer for 15 minutes. Combine cornstarch with cold water in a small bowl; gradually add to soup, stirring constantly. Stir in chicken and noodles; heat through, about 5 to 10 minutes.

★ GIFT IT ★ Tuck a jar of Grandma's Chicken Noodle Soup in a basket with a farmhouse bowl, a loaf of freshly baked bread and sweet creamy butter. A warm-hearted gift on a chilly winter's day!

Grandma's Chicken Noodle Soup

**Chris McCain,** Mosinee, WI

# Chicken-Tortellini Soup

Substitute this version with cheese tortellini for ordinary chicken noodle soup. It's just as easy and equally soothing.

### Makes 6 servings

1 lb. boneless, skinless chicken
   breasts, cooked and cubed
9-oz. pkg. cheese tortellini,
   uncooked
46-oz. can chicken broth
1 c. carrots, peeled and chopped
1/2 c. onion, chopped
1/2 c. celery, sliced
1/2 t. dried thyme
1/4 t. pepper
1 bay leaf

Combine all ingredients in a stockpot; bring to a boil over medium heat. Reduce heat, cover and simmer until tortellini is tender. Discard bay leaf.

**Marian Forck,** Chamois, MO

# Creamy Chicken & Macaroni Soup

A friend made this soup and let me sample it...I loved it! It is a filling soup and great with homemade bread.

### Makes 8 servings

2 c. cooked chicken, chopped
16-oz. pkg. frozen mixed vegetables
2 c. chicken broth
10-3/4 oz. can cream of chicken soup
3/4 c. celery, chopped
2 T. dried parsley, or to taste
2 cubes chicken bouillon
20-oz. pkg. frozen macaroni &
   cheese dinner

Combine all ingredients except macaroni & cheese dinner in a slow cooker. Cover and cook on low setting for 4 hours. Add frozen macaroni & cheese. Cover and cook for an additional 2 hours on low setting, stirring occasionally.

Chicken-Tortellini Soup

**Rogene Rogers,** Bemidji, MN

# Raspberry & Chicken Salad

We can't wait for raspberry season so we can pick basketfuls ourselves! I like to serve this salad with fresh-baked muffins.

*Makes 4 servings*

1 c. white wine or chicken broth
1 c. water
4 boneless, skinless chicken breasts
1/3 c. olive oil
3 T. raspberry vinegar
1/2 t. Dijon mustard
salt and pepper to taste
10-oz. pkg. mixed salad greens
1 pt. fresh raspberries

Combine wine or chicken broth and water in a saucepan over medium heat. Cover; bring to a boil. Reduce heat to medium-low and add chicken. Cover and simmer for 10 minutes, or until cooked through; drain. Let chicken cool and cut into 1/4-inch slices. Combine olive oil, vinegar, mustard, salt and pepper in a small screw-top jar; shake well. In a large bowl, toss salad greens with 1/3 of dressing. In a blender, blend remaining dressing with 1/3 cup of raspberries until smooth. Arrange salad on individual serving plates; top with chicken and remaining raspberries. Drizzle with dressing; serve immediately.

★ SIMPLE INGREDIENT SWAP ★
**Fresh blueberries, blackberries and strawberries would be just as delicious in this salad!**

**Raspberry & Chicken Salad**

**Vickie,** Gooseberry Patch

# BBQ Beef & Wagon Wheels Salad

A hearty salad for cowboy-size appetites.

### Makes 4 servings

1 c. wagon wheel pasta, uncooked
1 c. deli roast beef, cut into thin strips
3/4 c. onion, sliced
1/2 c. green pepper, chopped
2/3 c. barbecue sauce
2 T. Dijon mustard
2 c. red leaf lettuce, torn
2 c. green leaf lettuce, torn
Garnish: 1 tomato, sliced

Cook pasta according to package directions; drain and rinse with cold water. Combine pasta, beef, onion and green pepper in a large bowl; set aside. In a small bowl, mix together barbecue sauce and mustard; stir into beef mixture. Cover and chill. At serving time, toss together lettuces; arrange on salad plates. Spoon beef mixture over lettuce; garnish with tomato slices.

**Darlene Marks,** Youngstown, OH

# Darlene's 5-Can Beef Stew

I've shared this slow-cooker recipe with just about everyone I know! We all love it because it's comforting and delicious as well as easy to fix. Just add a fresh salad and some hearty bread.

### Serves 4 to 6

1 lb. stew beef cubes
14-1/2 oz. can diced tomatoes
14-1/2 oz. can green beans
15-1/4 oz. can corn
14-1/2 oz. can sliced carrots
14-1/2 oz. can diced new potatoes
1 c. brewed coffee
1-oz. pkg. onion soup mix

Place beef in a slow cooker. Pour all vegetables, without draining, over top. Add coffee to slow cooker; sprinkle soup mix over all. Mix gently with a large spoon. Cover and cook on low setting for 8 hours.

**BBQ Beef & Wagon Wheels Salad**

**Sarah Cline,** Las Vegas, NV

# Rich & Meaty Chili

Don't forget all the good things that go with this...hearty crackers, golden cornbread or thick slices of homebaked bread. Yum!

*Makes 8 servings*

1 lb. lean ground beef
1/2 c. onion, chopped
1 T. butter
2  15-1/2 oz. cans no-salt kidney beans
2  15-oz. cans no-salt chili beans
4 c. tomatoes, diced
6-oz. can tomato paste
1-1/2 c. water
1 c. celery, chopped
1 c. green pepper, chopped

2 to 3 t. chili powder
1/2 t. dried oregano
1/2 t. salt
1/4 t. pepper
1/8 t. hot pepper sauce
1 bay leaf

In a Dutch oven over medium-high heat, brown beef with onion in butter; drain. Stir in remaining ingredients. Bring to a boil; reduce heat to low. Simmer for one hour, stirring occasionally. Remove bay leaf before serving.

★ TIME-SAVING SHORTCUT ★ Turn leftovers into plan-overs! When you create the week's menu, plan two meals that use some of the same ingredients. Extra baked chicken can become shredded chicken sandwiches another night...extra chili can turn into chili dogs. The possibilities are endless and real time-savers.

Rich & Meaty Chili

**Beth Smith,** Manchester, MI

# Mexican Chicken Chili

My sister-in-law Penny made this slow-cooker stew for a gathering and it has become my son Nathan's favorite soup.

### Makes 6 servings

3 to 4 boneless, skinless chicken
   breasts
2  15-oz. cans Great Northern
   beans, drained
15-oz. can hominy, drained
4-oz. can chopped green chiles
10-3/4 oz. can low-sodium cream
   of mushroom soup
1-1/4 oz. pkg. taco seasoning mix
**Optional: milk or chicken broth**
**Garnish: nacho cheese-flavored**
   **tortilla chips**

Place chicken in a 4-quart slow cooker. Layer with beans, hominy, chiles and soup; sprinkle taco seasoning over top. Cover and cook on low setting for 7 to 8 hours. Do not peek and do not stir during cooking. At serving time, use a spoon to break up chicken; stir. If chili is too thick, add a little milk or chicken broth to desired consistency. Serve with tortilla chips.

**Angela Bissette,** Middlesex, NC

# White Bean Chicken Chili

This recipe is both delicious and easy to prepare. Add a crisp tossed salad and homemade crusty bread for a complete meal.

### Makes 8 servings

4 boneless chicken thighs, cooked
   and diced
2  15-oz. cans Great Northern beans
10-3/4 oz. can cream of chicken soup
32-oz. container chicken broth
10-oz. can diced tomatoes with green
   chiles
**Garnish: shredded Cheddar cheese,**
   **sour cream**

In a large soup pot, combine chicken, undrained beans, soup, broth and tomatoes. Bring to a boil over medium-high heat. Reduce heat to medium-low. Simmer, stirring occasionally, for 30 to 45 minutes. Garnish individual servings as desired.

★ TIME-SAVING SHORTCUT ★

Chicken thighs are extra flavorful and easy on the budget, but are usually sold with the bone in. To speed up cooking time, use a sharp knife to make a deep cut on each side of the bone.

**Mexican Chicken Chili**

**Connie Hilty,** Pearland, TX

# French Onion Beef Stew

This scrumptious soup is a breeze to toss together for a simple Sunday meal.

### Makes 4 servings

14-1/2 oz. can chicken broth
1 c. apple juice
4 carrots, peeled and sliced
2 onions, thinly sliced
8 sprigs fresh thyme
1-1/2 lbs. stew beef cubes
salt and pepper to taste
3 T. all-purpose flour
4 thick slices French bread
1 c. Gruyère cheese, shredded

Combine chicken broth, apple juice, carrots, onions and thyme in a slow cooker; set aside. Sprinkle beef with salt, pepper and flour; toss to coat well. Add beef to slow cooker; mix well. Cover and cook on low setting for 8 hours. Just before serving, place bread slices on a baking sheet; sprinkle evenly with cheese. Broil for one to 2 minutes, until cheese is melted and golden. Spoon stew into bowls; top each with a cheese toast.

French Onion Beef Stew

**Jean DePerna,** Fairport, NY

# Tuscan Beef Stew

One morning I tossed a few things together and this delicious dish was the result. I have been asked to make it ever since!

*Makes 6 servings*

2 lbs. stew beef cubes
2 to 3 T. oil
1/2 c. dry red wine or water
2 16-oz. cans cannellini beans, drained and rinsed
14-1/2 oz. can Italian-style diced tomatoes
3 carrots, peeled and cut into 1-inch pieces
1 t. Italian seasoning
1/2 t. garlic powder
15-oz. can tomato sauce
10-1/2 oz. can beef broth

In a large skillet over medium-high heat, cook beef in oil until no longer pink in the center; drain and transfer to a slow cooker. Add remaining ingredients. Cover and cook on low setting for 8 to 9 hours.

**Lori Rosenberg,** University Heights, OH

# Burger Barley Soup

In our family, the first batch of this soup signals the arrival of cooler weather.

*Serves 10 to 12*

1-1/2 lbs. lean ground beef
28-oz. can diced tomatoes
8-oz. can tomato sauce
1/2 c. catsup
6 c. water
2 c. carrots, peeled and sliced
1-1/2 c. onion, chopped
1-1/2 c. celery, chopped
1/2 c. green pepper, chopped
1/2 c. pearl barley, uncooked
1 T. beef bouillon granules
1 T. salt
1/8 t. pepper
2 bay leaves

In a Dutch oven over medium heat, brown beef until no longer pink; drain. Remove beef from pot; rinse in a colander. Return beef to pot; stir in tomatoes with juice and remaining ingredients. Bring to a boil. Reduce heat; cover and simmer for one hour, or until vegetables and barley are tender. Remove bay leaves before serving.

Tuscan Beef Stew

**Sandy Roy,** Crestwood, KY

# Reuben Soup

Looking for a creamy soup that really sticks to your ribs? This is it!

*Makes 6 servings*

2 T. butter
1 onion, chopped
4 c. chicken broth
1 c. sauerkraut, drained and chopped
1 bay leaf
2 T. cornstarch
1/4 c. cold water
1 c. whipping cream
1 c. half-and-half
1 lb. deli corned beef, cubed
1 c. shredded Swiss cheese
salt and white pepper to taste
Garnish: rye croutons

Melt butter in a saucepan over medium heat. Add onion and cook until soft. Add chicken broth, sauerkraut and bay leaf. Cover; reduce heat to medium-low and simmer for 15 minutes. In a small bowl, mix cornstarch and water; add to saucepan. Stir in cream, half-and-half, corned beef and cheese. Simmer over very low heat for 10 to 15 minutes, stirring often; do not boil. Remove bay leaf and season with salt and pepper. Ladle into bowls and sprinkle with croutons.

★ SIMPLE INGREDIENT SWAP ★ **Top bowls of hot soup with plain or cheesy popcorn instead of croutons for a crunchy surprise.**

Reuben Soup

**Janis Parr,** Ontario, Canada

# Village Stone Soup

I love the folktale story of Stone Soup. It has wonderful meaning and is a lesson for all. This soup inspired by the tale will warm you through & through.

### Makes 12 servings

4 14-1/2 oz. cans chicken broth
5 potatoes, peeled and cubed
1 small butternut squash, peeled and
    coarsely chopped
4 carrots, peeled and coarsely
    chopped
1 onion, coarsely chopped
1 c. celery, coarsely chopped
1/2 c. quick-cooking barley, uncooked
salt and pepper to taste
3 cubes chicken bouillon
3-1/2 c. cooked chicken, cubed
14-1/2 oz. can diced tomatoes
1 c. fresh or frozen green peas

In a large soup pot over high heat, combine chicken broth, potatoes, squash, carrots, onion and celery. Bring to a boil; reduce heat to medium-low. Cover and simmer for 20 to 25 minutes, until vegetables are tender, stirring occasionally. Add barley, seasonings, bouillon cubes, chicken, tomatoes with juice and peas. Return heat to high; bring to a boil. Reduce heat to medium-low; cover and simmer for 12 to 15 minutes, until barley is tender. Serve piping hot.

★ SPICY SECRET ★ Treat yourself to crisp savory crackers with soup. Spread saltines with softened butter, then sprinkle lightly with chili powder, paprika or another favorite spice. Pop into a 350-degree oven just until golden, 3 to 6 minutes.

Village Stone Soup

**Jill Burton,** Gooseberry Patch

# Mexican Chicken & Avocado Salad

Sometimes I serve this over a bed of lettuce, and sometimes over a cup of chilled rice flavored with a squeeze of lime juice. So fresh tasting!

### Serves 4 to 6

2 c. deli roast chicken, boned and
   shredded
15-oz. can black beans, drained
   and rinsed
15-oz. can shoepeg corn, drained
1 avocado, halved, pitted and diced
6 green onions, thinly sliced
2 c. tomatoes, chopped, or grape
   tomatoes, halved
Optional: 1/2 c. chopped fresh
   cilantro
1/2 c. citrus vinaigrette salad
   dressing
salt and pepper to taste

In a large bowl, combine chicken, beans, corn, avocado, onions, tomatoes and cilantro, if using. Pour vinaigrette over salad; add salt and pepper to taste. Stir salad to coat vegetables with dressing; cover and chill until serving.

**Megan Sabo,** Daytona Beach, FL

# Megan's Crazy Spicy Chili

Mom gave me this easy chili recipe when I was learning to cook. After I'd made it for awhile, I decided to add a couple of things and now I have a spicy new version that's my very own.

### Serves 6 to 8

1 lb. ground beef
1 onion, chopped
1/2 lb. spicy ground pork sausage
1/2 lb. andouille pork link sausage,
   sliced
2  15-1/2 oz. cans red kidney beans
2  14-1/2 oz. cans diced tomatoes
2  8-oz. cans tomato sauce
1 c. frozen corn
1-1/2 c. water
1-1/4 oz. pkg. chili seasoning mix
Garnish: sour cream, shredded
   Cheddar cheese, corn chips

In a large soup pot over medium-high heat, brown beef and onion; drain and set aside in a bowl. In the same pot, brown spicy sausage and andouille together; drain. Add beef mixture, undrained beans, undrained tomatoes and remaining ingredients except garnish. Reduce heat to low and simmer for about one hour, stirring occasionally. Serve in individual bowls topped with sour cream, cheese and corn chips.

Mexican Chicken & Avocado Salad

**Charlotte Smith,** Alexandria, PA

# Bread Bowl Beef Stew

A great recipe for a cool, rainy day. Easy and yummy!

### Makes 8 servings

1 t. oil
1 lb. boneless top sirloin steak, cubed
3/4 t. garlic salt
1/4 t. pepper
.87-oz. pkg. brown gravy mix
1-1/3 c. water
2 to 3 potatoes, peeled, cooked and quartered
9-oz. pkg. frozen baby carrots, thawed and drained
1-1/2 c. frozen sweet peas, thawed and drained
1 c. canned whole pearl onions, drained
8-oz. tube refrigerated large buttermilk biscuits, room temperature

Heat oil in a skillet over medium to high heat. Add beef and cook until browned. Add seasonings, dry gravy mix and water. Bring to a boil, stirring constantly. Add vegetables. Simmer for 5 minutes; set aside. Separate biscuits and flatten to 5-1/2 inch rounds. Press firmly into 8 greased jumbo muffin cups, forming a 1/4-inch rim. Spoon 3/4 cup beef mixture into each cup. Bake, uncovered, at 350 degrees for 14 minutes. Cover with aluminum foil and bake an additional 8 minutes.

★ HOT TIP ★ When frying chicken or browning beef for stew, you'll get the best results if the pan isn't overcrowded. Use an extra large skillet or cook in two batches.

**Bread Bowl Beef Stew**

**Carol Hickman,** Kingsport, TN

# Island Chicken Salad

Pile this delicious chicken salad high on a lettuce leaf or serve on fresh croissants for a quick sandwich.

### Makes 4 servings

10-oz. can chunk white chicken, drained
8-oz. can crushed pineapple, drained
2 stalks celery, diced
1/2 c. cream cheese, softened
2 T. mayonnaise
Garnish: sliced almonds

In a large bowl, combine all ingredients except almonds. Mix together until well blended. Cover and chill; serve topped with almonds. Makes 4 servings.

**Michelle Powell,** Valley, AL

# Cure-All Chicken Soup

This simple soup clears your sniffles and soothes your heart as it tickles your tastebuds!

### Makes 10 servings

4 chicken breasts
12 c. water
2 15-oz. cans diced tomatoes with green chiles
2 10-oz. pkgs. frozen creamed corn, thawed
1 c. milk
salt and pepper to taste

In a stockpot, combine chicken and water. Simmer over medium-low heat until chicken is tender. Remove chicken to a plate, reserving broth in pot. Add tomatoes with juice and corn to reserved broth. Dice chicken and add to broth, discarding skin and bones. Simmer over low heat for 2 hours. Stir in milk without boiling; season with salt and pepper.

Island Chicken Salad

**LuAnn Tracy,** Aliquippa, PA

# Italian Wedding Soup

I got this wonderful recipe from my sister's daughter-in-law. Serve with a tangy salad and bread sticks for a simple meal.

### Serves 6 to 8

**25 frozen cooked Italian meatballs**
**6 c. chicken broth**
**1 c. boneless, skinless chicken breast, chopped**
**1/2 c. carrot, peeled and diced**
**1/2 c. celery, diced**
**1 bunch spinach, torn**
**garlic salt to taste**
**1/4 c. grated Parmesan-Romano cheese**
**1/4 c. ditalini pasta, uncooked**
**Garnish: additional grated Parmesan-Romano cheese**

Combine all ingredients except pasta and garnish in a slow cooker. Cover and cook on low setting for 7 to 8 hours. About 20 minutes before serving, cook pasta according to package directions; drain and stir into slow cooker. Sprinkle servings with a little more cheese.

★ HOT TIP ★ To serve alongside Italian Wedding Soup, turn leftover hot dog buns into garlic bread sticks in a jiffy. Spread buns with softened butter, sprinkle with garlic salt and broil until toasty!

Italian Wedding Soup

**Amanda Dixon,** Dublin, OH

# Tarragon Steak Dinner Salad

Delicious...a perfect light summer meal.

### Makes 4 servings

6 c. Boston lettuce
2 pears, peeled, cored and sliced
1/2 red onion, thinly sliced
1/2 lb. grilled beef steak, thinly sliced
1/4 c. crumbled blue cheese
1/2 c. red wine vinaigrette salad dressing
1 T. fresh tarragon, minced
1/4 t. pepper

Arrange lettuce, pears and onion on 4 serving plates. Top with sliced steak and sprinkle with cheese. Combine dressing, tarragon and pepper in a small bowl; whisk well. Drizzle dressing mixture over salad.

**Cynthia Johnson,** Verona, WI

# Beefy Vegetable Soup

This slow-cooker soup is so easy to put together. It's delicious and makes your home smell wonderful, especially on chilly fall nights!

### Makes 8 servings

1 lb. ground beef
1 onion, chopped
1 clove garlic, minced
16-oz. can kidney beans
16-oz. can cannellini beans
10-oz. pkg. frozen corn & pea blend
14-1/2 oz. can diced tomatoes
2  8-oz. cans tomato sauce
1 c. carrots, peeled and shredded
1 t. chili powder
1/2 t. dried basil
1/2 t. salt
1/4 t. pepper

In a skillet, cook beef, onion and garlic over medium heat until beef is no longer pink; drain. Transfer to a 5-quart slow cooker. Add remaining ingredients; mix well. Cover and cook on low setting for 8 hours, or until thick and bubbly.

**Tarragon Steak Dinner Salad**

**Andrea Pocreva,** San Antonio, TX

# White Chicken Chili

This chili recipe feeds a crowd! If you're hosting a smaller group, it is easily halved.

### Serves 16 to 20

2 onions, chopped
1 T. olive oil
6 c. chicken broth
6 15-1/2 oz. cans Great Northern
   beans, drained and rinsed
3 5-oz. cans chicken, drained
2 4-oz. cans diced green chiles
2 t. ground cumin
1 t. garlic powder
1-1/2 t. dried oregano
1/4 t. white pepper
12-oz. container sour cream
3 c. shredded Monterey Jack cheese

In a large stockpot over medium heat, sauté onions in oil until tender. Stir in remaining ingredients except sour cream and cheese. Simmer for 30 minutes, stirring frequently, until heated through. Shortly before serving time, add sour cream and cheese. Stir until cheese is melted.

★ TIME-SAVING SHORTCUT ★ A full pantry is so reassuring! With pasta, rice, dried beans, favorite sauces, baking mixes and canned meat, soups, veggies and fruit on hand, you're all set to stir up a satisfying meal anytime.

White Chicken Chili

**Regina Vining,** Warwick, RI

# ABC Chicken Soup

My kids are so busy spelling their names in this soup, they don't realize they're eating veggies!

### Serves 8 to 10

1 onion, chopped
2 carrots, peeled and chopped
2 stalks celery, chopped
1 T. oil
2 cloves garlic, minced
2 32-oz. containers chicken broth
2 c. cooked chicken, shredded
1/4 t. dried thyme
salt and pepper to taste
1/2 c. alphabet-shaped pasta, uncooked

In a Dutch oven over medium-high heat, sauté onion, carrots and celery in hot oil for 5 minutes. Add garlic and sauté one minute. Stir in broth, chicken and seasonings. Bring to a boil. Reduce heat and simmer 15 minutes, stirring occasionally. Add pasta and cook 8 minutes, until tender.

**Panda Spurgin,** Berryville, AR

# Chicken Enchilada Chili

I always use bone-in chicken thighs or legs...I find the flavor is so much better. Serve with cornbread or corn chips.

### Makes 10 servings

2  15-oz. cans pinto beans, black beans, chili beans or a combination
2  14-1/2 oz. cans diced tomatoes
2  10-oz. cans enchilada sauce
1 c. celery, diced
1 onion, diced
1 to 2 T. chili powder
1 t. ground cumin
4 chicken thighs and/or legs, skin removed
Garnish: sour cream, shredded Cheddar cheese, diced avocado, chopped fresh cilantro

In a slow cooker, combine undrained beans, undrained tomatoes, enchilada sauce, vegetables and seasonings. Stir gently; place chicken pieces on top. Cover and cook on low setting for 8 hours. Remove chicken to a plate and shred, discarding bones. Return chicken to slow cooker; stir. Serve garnished with desired toppings.

ABC Chicken Soup

**Jeanne Dinnel,** Canby, OR

# Chicken Enchilada Soup

This recipe may look lengthy, but it goes together in a jiffy! Serve it with a simple salad of ripe tomato and avocado drizzled with lime vinaigrette dressing.

### Makes 6 servings

1 onion, chopped
1 clove garlic, pressed
1 to 2 t. oil
14-1/2 oz. can beef broth
14-1/2 oz. can chicken broth
10-3/4 oz. can cream of chicken soup
1-1/2 c. water
12-1/2 oz. can chicken, drained
4-oz. can chopped green chiles
2 t. Worcestershire sauce
1 T. steak sauce
1 t. ground cumin
1 t. chili powder
1/8 t. pepper
6 corn tortillas, cut into strips
1 c. shredded Cheddar cheese

In a stockpot over medium heat, sauté onion and garlic in oil. Add remaining ingredients except tortilla strips and cheese; bring to a boil. Cover; reduce heat and simmer for one hour, stirring occasionally. Uncover; stir in tortilla strips and cheese. Simmer an additional 10 minutes.

★ SAVVY SIDE ★ A fun new way to serve cornbread...waffle wedges! Mix up the batter, thin it slightly with a little extra milk, then bake in a waffle iron until crisp. Terrific for dunking in soup or chili!

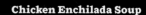
Chicken Enchilada Soup

**Janelle Dixon,** Fernley, NV

# Creamy White Chili

This chili has such fabulous flavor with its blend of green chiles, cumin, sour cream and chicken.

*Serves 6 to 8*

1 T. oil
1 lb. boneless, skinless chicken
   breasts, cubed
1 onion, chopped
14-oz. can chicken broth
2  15.8-oz. cans Great Northern
   beans, drained and rinsed
2  4-1/2 oz. cans chopped green
   chiles, undrained
1-1/2 t. garlic powder
1 t. salt
1 t. ground cumin
1/2 t. dried oregano
8-oz. container sour cream
1 c. whipping cream
2 c. shredded Monterey Jack cheese
Garnish: fresh cilantro sprigs

Heat oil in a large skillet over medium heat; add chicken and onion. Sauté 10 minutes or until chicken is done; set aside. Combine broth, beans, chiles and seasonings in a large Dutch oven. Bring to a boil over medium-high heat. Add chicken mixture; reduce heat and simmer 30 minutes. Add sour cream and whipping cream, stirring well. Top each serving with shredded cheese; garnish with cilantro, as desired.

★ HOT TIP ★ A hometown chili cook-off! Ask neighbors to bring a pot of their best "secret recipe" chili to share, then have a friendly judging for the best. You provide lots of crackers and buttered cornbread, chilled cider and bright red bandannas for terrific lap-size napkins.

Creamy White Chili

**Alice Hardin,** Antioch, CA

# Italian Meatball Soup

Sprinkle with freshly shredded Parmesan cheese for added flavor.

### Serves 4 to 6

16-oz. pkg. frozen Italian-style
   meatballs
2  14-1/2 oz. cans diced tomatoes
   with Italian herbs
2  14-1/2 oz. cans beef broth
1 c. potato, peeled and diced
1/2 c. onion, chopped
1/4 t. garlic pepper
16-oz. pkg. frozen mixed vegetables

In a slow cooker, mix frozen meatballs, tomatoes with juice, beef broth, potato, onion and garlic pepper. Cover and cook on low setting for 8 to 10 hours. Stir in frozen vegetables. Increase setting to high; cover and cook for one additional hour, or until vegetables are tender.

**Diane Hixon,** Niceville, FL

# Slow-Cooked Campfire Stew

I used to have a small cafe and one day I made this stew to serve. It was a big hit...even folks who said they didn't like corn or butter beans enjoyed it!

### Serves 6 to 8

3 potatoes, peeled and diced
1 onion, chopped
2  16-oz. cans stewed tomatoes
16-oz. can butter beans
16-oz. can creamed corn
14-1/2 oz. container shredded BBQ
   beef
14-1/2 oz. container shredded BBQ
   pork
1 T. Worcestershire sauce
1 T. lemon juice
salt and pepper to taste

In a saucepan, cover potatoes and onion with water. Cook over medium-high heat for 10 to 15 minutes, until tender. Drain, reserving 1/4 cup cooking liquid. Add potatoes, onion and reserved liquid to a slow cooker along with undrained canned vegetables and remaining ingredients. Stir well; cover and cook on low setting for 4 hours.

**Italian Meatball Soup**

**Peggy Cantrell,** Okmulgee, OK

# Unstuffed Green Pepper Soup

This soup is right up there on my list of comfort foods! All the flavors of a stuffed green pepper without the work.

### Makes 8 servings

2 lbs. ground beef
2  10-3/4 oz. cans tomato soup
28-oz. can petite diced tomatoes
4-oz. can mushroom pieces, drained
2 c. green peppers, diced
1 c. onion, diced
1/4 c. brown sugar, packed
3 to 4 c. beef broth
2 c. cooked rice

In a stockpot over medium heat, brown ground beef; drain. Stir in soup, vegetables and brown sugar. Add desired amount of beef broth. Simmer, covered, until peppers and onion are tender, about 30 minutes. Stir in rice about 5 minutes before serving.

★ TIME-SAVING SHORTCUT ★ A soup supper is warm and comforting on a chilly night...it's so easy to prepare too. Just add a basket of muffins and a crock of sweet butter. Dinner is served!

Unstuffed Green Pepper Soup

**Jocelyn Medina,** Phoenixville, PA

# Beef Stew & Biscuits

This tried & true one-pot meal is perfect for Sunday dinner.

### *Serves 4 to 6*

1 lb. ground beef
1/4 c. onion, chopped
1/4 t. dried basil
1/8 t. pepper
3-1/2 c. frozen or canned mixed
 vegetables
2  8-oz. cans tomato sauce
1 c. sharp Cheddar cheese, cubed
12-oz. tube refrigerated biscuits

In a skillet, brown beef and onion; drain. Add seasonings, mixed vegetables and tomato sauce; mix well. Cover and simmer for 5 minutes. Fold in cheese cubes; pour into an ungreased 2-quart casserole dish. Arrange biscuits on top. Bake, uncovered, at 375 degrees for 25 minutes, or until biscuits are golden.

★ DOUBLE DUTY ★ Biscuit toppers make a hearty meal of any bowl of thick soup or stew. Flatten jumbo refrigerated biscuits and arrange on an ungreased baking sheet. Pierce several times with a fork and bake as package directs. Place each topper on a bowl of hot, bubbly soup and serve.

**Beef Stew & Biscuits**

**Pat Beach,** Fisherville, KY

# Slow-Cooked Veggie-Beef Soup

For someone who couldn't even boil water when she got married, my daughter Toni is a fabulous cook! She says all it takes to be a great cook is a good, full-flavored recipe like this one.

### Serves 10 to 12

1 to 1-1/2 lbs. stew beef cubes
46-oz. can cocktail vegetable juice
2 c. water
5 cubes beef bouillon
1/2 onion, chopped
2 to 3 potatoes, peeled and cubed
3 c. cabbage, shredded
16-oz. pkg. frozen mixed vegetables

Combine all ingredients in a slow cooker. Cover and cook on low setting for 8 to 9 hours, until all ingredients are tender.

**Vickie,** Gooseberry Patch

# Mexican Vegetable Soup

Looking for a something a little different from chili? Try this!

### Makes 10 servings

1 lb. ground beef
1-1/4 oz. pkg. taco seasoning mix
46-oz. can tomato juice
12-oz. can tomato paste
16-oz. pkg frozen mixed vegetables
15-oz. can chili with hot beans
Garnish: shredded Cheddar cheese, crushed corn chips

In a Dutch oven, brown beef over medium heat; drain. Add remaining ingredients except garnish; bring just to a boil. Reduce heat to low. Simmer for 20 to 25 minutes, until vegetables are tender, stirring occasionally. Top each serving with cheese and corn chips.

Slow-Cooked Veggie-Beef Soup

**Jo Ann,** Gooseberry Patch

# Beef & Butternut Stew

I always grow some butternut squash in my garden every year. I love to give them away to friends & neighbors...but I really love making this delicious stew with them!

### Serves 8 to 10

2 t. dried thyme
2 t. salt
3/4 t. pepper
5 T. cornstarch
1-1/2 lb. beef round roast, cubed
1 bulb fennel, sliced
3/4 lb. redskin potatoes, quartered
28-oz. can whole tomatoes, drained and tomatoes halved
1 butternut squash, peeled, seeded and cubed
1 t. olive oil

Combine seasonings in a bowl; reserve one teaspoon seasoning mixture. Combine cornstarch with remaining seasoning mixture. Toss beef, fennel and potatoes in cornstarch mixture until well coated. Transfer beef mixture to a slow cooker; spoon tomatoes over top. In a separate bowl, toss squash with oil and reserved spice mixture. Layer squash on top of tomatoes. Cover and cook on low setting for 8 hours.

★ SIMPLE INGREDIENT SWAP ★
**Butternut squash seeds can be toasted just like pumpkin seeds! Rinse seeds and pat dry, then toss with olive oil and coarse salt. Spread on an ungreased baking sheet and bake for 12 to 15 minutes at 350 degrees, until golden. Cool and enjoy.**

Beef & Butternut Stew

**Rita Morgan,** Pueblo, CO

# Hearty Hominy Beef Stew

We like to top our soup with some sliced avocado for extra flavor and a little more creaminess.

### Makes 6 servings

1 onion, chopped
2-lb. beef chuck roast, cubed
1/4 t. salt
1 green pepper, chopped
3 carrots, peeled and sliced
3 stalks celery, sliced
3 cloves garlic, minced
14-1/2 oz. can petite diced tomatoes
1 c. beef broth, divided
2 T. cornstarch
15-oz. can hominy, drained and
   rinsed

Place onion in a lightly greased slow cooker; top with beef. Sprinkle with salt. Add green pepper, carrots, celery and garlic to slow cooker. Pour tomatoes with juice and 3/4 cup broth over all. Cover and cook on low setting for 8 hours. In a bowl, mix together cornstarch and remaining broth until smooth; stir into slow cooker during the last 15 minutes of cooking. Stir in hominy and heat through.

★ SIMPLE INGREDIENT SWAP ★ **If your pantry is out of hominy, swap it out for an equal amount of canned corn.**

**Hearty Hominy Beef Stew**

**Romaine Chicken Caesar Wraps, Page 150**

# CHAPTER THREE

# Sandwiches

**Bacon-Stuffed Burgers, Page 136**

**Yiayia's Chicken Pitas, Page 176**

**Janice Pigga,** Bethlehem, PA

# Red Pepper & Chicken Bagels

This is a quick recipe that's perfect whenever time is short.

### Makes 2 servings

2 boneless, skinless chicken breasts
1/8 t. salt
1/8 t. pepper
1/4 c. balsamic vinegar
3 T. Worcestershire sauce
2 bagels, split
2 slices fresh mozzarella cheese
2 slices roasted red pepper

Place chicken between 2 pieces of wax paper; pound until thin. Sprinkle with salt and pepper. In a bowl, combine vinegar and Worcestershire sauce; add chicken and marinate for 10 to 15 minutes. Drain and discard marinade. Place chicken on a lightly greased grill or in a skillet over medium heat. Cook and turn until chicken is golden and juices run clear, about 20 minutes. Place chicken on 2 bagel halves; top with cheese and pepper slices. Add remaining bagel halves. Arrange sandwiches on an ungreased baking sheet. Bake at 350 degrees until cheese is melted, about 5 to 10 minutes.

**Heather Porter,** Villa Park, IL

# Chicago Italian Beef

If you come from Chicago you know Italian beef! Serve with chewy, delicious Italian rolls and top with some of the gravy from the slow cooker...the taste is out of this world!

### Serves 8 to 16

4 to 5-lb. beef rump roast or bottom round roast
16-oz. jar pepperoncini
16-oz. jar mild giardiniera mix in oil
14-oz. can beef broth
1.05-oz. pkg. Italian salad dressing mix
8 to 16 Italian rolls, split

Place roast in a large slow cooker. Top with undrained pepperoncini and giardeniera; pour in broth and sprinkle with dressing mix. Cover and cook on low setting for 6 to 8 hours. Reserving liquid in slow cooker, shred beef with 2 forks. To serve, top rolls with beef and some of the liquid and vegetables from slow cooker.

Red Pepper & Chicken Bagels

**Lea Ann Burwell,** Charles Town, WV

# Ranch Chicken Wraps

My husband and children just love these easy-to-make wraps and request them often.

### Makes 8 to 10 wraps

1/2 t. oil
4 boneless, skinless chicken breasts,
    cut into strips
2.8-oz. can French fried onions
1/4 c. bacon bits
8-oz. pkg. shredded Cheddar cheese
1 bunch leaf lettuce, separated
8 to 10  8-inch flour tortillas
Garnish: ranch salad dressing

Heat oil in a large non-stick skillet over medium heat; add chicken. Cook until chicken is golden and juices run clear when pierced. Add onions, bacon bits and cheese to skillet; cook over low heat until cheese melts. Place several lettuce leaves on each tortilla and spoon chicken mixture down the center; roll up. Serve with ranch salad dressing.

★ TIME-SAVING SHORTCUT ★ A roast chicken from the deli is the busy cook's secret ingredient! The chicken is already cooked and ready for whatever recipe you decide to make.

**Ranch Chicken Wraps**

Luna Gabriel, Belmont, MA

# Cranberry-Chicken Quesadillas

A quick-fix meal the whole family will love! Substitute leftover turkey for a terrific post-holiday meal.

### Makes 6 servings

4 8-inch flour tortillas
2 c. cooked chicken, shredded
1-1/2 c. whole-berry cranberry sauce
8-oz. pkg. shredded Mexican-blend cheese
2 t. pepper
1/2 t. garlic powder, or to taste
Optional: salsa verde, sour cream

Spray a 13"x9" baking pan generously with non-stick vegetable spray. Place 2 tortillas in the pan, side by side. Layer chicken, cranberry sauce and cheese evenly over tortillas; sprinkle with seasonings. Spray remaining tortillas on both sides with non-stick spray; arrange over ingredients in pan. Bake, uncovered, at 350 degrees for 30 to 35 minutes, until heated through and cheese is melted. Serve topped with salsa verde and sour cream, if desired.

Jenn Erickson, Pacific Grove, CA

# Sesame Chicken Tea Sandwiches

These elegant little tea sandwiches are a wonderful addition to a classic tea party, shower or brunch, and even to your child's lunchbox. My daughters Maddie and Mackenzie love them! It's a wonderful way to use leftover chicken.

### Makes 40 mini sandwiches

3 c. cooked chicken, finely chopped
1 c. light mayonnaise, divided
1/4 c. celery, inner stalk and leaves, minced
2 t. sesame oil
1/4 c. sliced almonds
salt and pepper to taste
20 slices soft whole-wheat sandwich bread
1/2 c. toasted sesame seed

In a bowl, combine chicken, 3/4 cup mayonnaise, celery and sesame oil. Crush almonds in your palm and add to bowl; stir to mix. Season with salt and pepper. For each sandwich, place a small scoop of chicken salad on a slice of bread. Top with another slice of bread; press lightly and trim crusts. Cut into 4 triangles on the diagonal. Using a butter knife, spread a thin layer of remaining mayonnaise along the sides of each tea sandwich; dip sandwich into sesame seed to coat mayonnaise.

Cranberry-Chicken Quesadillas

**Molly Cool,** Delaware, OH

# Bacon-Stuffed Burgers

These go so fast that I have to double the recipe!

### Makes 8 sandwiches

4 slices bacon
1/4 c. onion, chopped
4-oz. can mushroom pieces,
　drained and diced
1 lb. ground beef
1 lb. ground pork sausage
1/4 c. grated Parmesan cheese
1/2 t. pepper
1/2 t. garlic powder
2 T. steak sauce
8 sandwich buns, split
Optional: lettuce leaves, tomato
　slices, provolone cheese slices

In a skillet over medium heat, cook bacon until crisp. Remove bacon to a plate, reserving 2 tablespoons drippings in skillet. Add onion to drippings and sauté until tender. Add crumbled bacon and mushrooms; heat through and set aside. Combine beef, sausage, Parmesan cheese, pepper, garlic powder and steak sauce in a large bowl. Mix well and shape into 16 patties. Spoon bacon mixture over 8 patties. Place remaining patties on top and press edges tightly to seal. Grill over medium coals to desired doneness. Serve on buns with lettuce, tomato and cheese, if desired.

★ SAVVY SIDE ★ A tasty apple coleslaw goes well with Bacon-Stuffed Burgers. Simply toss together a large bag of coleslaw mix and a chopped Granny Smith apple. Stir in coleslaw dressing or mayonnaise to desired consistency.

Bacon-Stuffed Burgers

Amy Hunt, Traphill, NC

# Sandwich on a Stick

Here's a simple snack to make for a picnic or party. Adjust the ingredients and quantity to suit your family's tastes.

### Makes 8 servings

1/2 lb. deli roast chicken, cubed
1/2 lb. deli roast turkey, cubed
1/2 lb. deli baked ham, cubed
1/2 lb. Cheddar cheese, cut into cubes
4 c. bread, cut into cubes
1 pt. cherry tomatoes
4 dill pickles, cut into chunks
8 wooden skewers
Garnish: mustard, spicy brown
  mustard, mayonnaise

Alternate all ingredients except condiments onto skewers. Garnish as desired. Makes 8 servings.

Linda Cook, Ontario, Canada

# Apple-Chicken Salad Sandwich

Many years ago, I used to work in downtown Toronto and I would frequent a certain sandwich shop. I loved its chicken salad sandwiches! I couldn't remember exactly what was in their chicken salad, but I think after a few tries I got pretty close.

### Makes 2 sandwiches

1 boneless, skinless chicken breast,
  grilled and cubed
2 T. mayonnaise, or to taste
1 T. sunflower kernels
1 T. dried cranberries
1/2 red onion, chopped
1 apple, cored and cubed
salt and pepper to taste
2 sandwich buns, split

Combine all ingredients except buns in a large bowl; stir well. Place buns, split-side up, under a broiler to toast. Fill buns evenly with chicken mixture.

Sandwich on a Stick

Vickie, Gooseberry Patch

# Hearty Chicken-Bacon Melts

A warm, melty open-face sandwich you need to eat with a fork!

### Makes 4 servings

4 boneless, skinless chicken breasts
1 onion, sliced
2 t. margarine
2 t. olive oil
4 slices bread, toasted
4 t. steak sauce
8 slices bacon, crisply cooked
1 c. shredded Cheddar cheese

Place chicken between pieces of wax paper and flatten to about 1/4-inch thickness. In a large skillet, cook onion in margarine and oil until softened. Remove onion from skillet. Add chicken to skillet; cook for about 7 to 9 minutes on each side, until cooked through. Place toasted bread slices on a large baking sheet; spread each slice with one teaspoon steak sauce. Top each with a chicken breast, 2 slices bacon, 1/4 of onion slices and 1/4 cup cheese. Broil 4 to 6 inches from heat for one to 2 minutes, until cheese is melted.

★ HOT TIP ★ Bacon is tasty, but can be messy to fry...so bake it instead. Arrange slices on a jelly-roll pan and bake at 350 degrees. It'll be crispy in about 15 minutes, plus no messy spatters!

**Hearty Chicken-Bacon Melts**

**Jennifer Catterino,** Pasadena, MD

# Simple Sloppy Joes

These sandwiches will be a winner with the family for their flavor and with Mom for their ease!

### Serves 6 to 8

1 lb. ground beef
1 onion, chopped
1 c. catsup
1/4 c. water
2 T. Worcestershire sauce
1/4 t. salt
1/4 t. pepper
6 to 8 sandwich buns
dill pickle slices

Cook ground beef and onion in a large skillet over medium-high heat, stirring until beef crumbles and is no longer pink; drain. Stir in catsup, water, Worcestershire sauce, salt and pepper; simmer 20 minutes, stirring frequently. Spoon onto buns; top with dill pickle slices.

**Melissa Dattoli,** Richmond, VA

# BBQ Chicken Melts

A tasty, quick dinner that can be prepared on the grill or in the oven. We like these sandwich-style, but you can serve the chicken without the buns if you prefer.

### Makes 4 sandwiches

4 boneless, skinless chicken breasts
1/2 c. barbecue sauce, divided
4 slices deli ham
4 slices provolone cheese
4 hamburger buns, split
Optional: mayonnaise to taste

Brush chicken breasts with half of the barbecue sauce. Place on a hot grill; cook on both sides until chicken juices run clear. May also be placed in a greased baking pan. Bake, uncovered, at 450 degrees for 20 to 25 minutes, turning once, until done. Brush chicken with remaining barbecue sauce. Top each with a slice of ham and a slice of cheese. Grill or bake just until cheese is melted. Serve on buns with a little mayonnaise, if desired.

BBQ Chicken Melts

**Amy Michalik,** Norwalk, IA

# Philly Cheesesteak Sandwiches

A hearty meal-on-a-bun...onion, garlic, green pepper and mushrooms spooned over layers of beef and topped with melted cheese.

*Makes 6 sandwiches*

2 T. butter
1 lb. beef top round or ribeye steak, thinly sliced
seasoned salt and pepper to taste
1 onion, sliced
1 clove garlic, minced
1 green pepper, thinly sliced
Optional: 1 c. sliced mushrooms
1 lb. provolone, Gouda or Swiss cheese, sliced
6 hoagie buns or baguettes, split

Melt butter in a skillet over medium heat until lightly golden. Add steak; sprinkle with seasonings and sauté just until browned. Add onion, garlic, green pepper and mushrooms, if desired; stir. Cover and simmer for 5 to 7 minutes, until onion and pepper are tender. Add additional salt and pepper to taste. Remove from heat; set aside. Place 2 to 3 cheese slices in each bun; top each with 2 to 3 tablespoonfuls of steak mixture. Top with additional cheese, if desired. Wrap each sandwich in aluminum foil; bake at 350 degrees for 10 to 15 minutes, until cheese is melted.

★ DOUBLE DUTY ★ Paper coffee filters are great for serving up hoagies, tacos, wraps and burgers...no spills, no mess and easy to hold!

Philly Cheesesteak Sandwiches

**Jill Ross,** Pickerington, OH

# BBQ Chicken Calzones

With a recipe this easy, it's a pleasure to have my children lend a hand in the kitchen!

### Makes 4 servings

12-oz. tube refrigerated pizza dough
3 c. cooked chicken, diced
1 c. barbecue sauce
1 c. shredded mozzarella cheese
1 egg, beaten
1 t. water

On a floured surface, roll dough to 1/2-inch thickness; cut into 2 rectangles and place on ungreased baking sheets. In a bowl, combine chicken and barbecue sauce. For each calzone, spoon half the chicken mixture onto one half of the dough. Top with half the cheese. Fold over dough and seal the edges. Mix together egg and water. Use a pastry brush to brush egg mixture over each calzone; use a knife to cut 3 slits in the tops. Bake at 400 degrees for 25 minutes, or until golden.

**Sheila Cottrell,** Cincinnati, OH

# Baked Chicken Sandwiches

Make these sandwiches ahead and freeze for those busy nights when you're short on time but you want a hot meal.

### Makes 15 servings

4 c. cooked chicken, diced
10-3/4 oz. can cream of mushroom soup
10-3/4 oz. can cream of chicken soup
3 T. onion, diced
8-oz. can water chestnuts, thinly sliced
1 loaf sliced bread
2 eggs, beaten
1 T. milk
6 to 8 c. potato chips, crushed
10-1/2 oz. can chicken gravy

Mix chicken, soups, onion and water chestnuts together. Spoon mixture onto bread slices and top with another slice. Wrap in freezer paper to freeze. When ready to eat, mix together eggs and milk; remove sandwiches from freezer wrap, dip in egg mixture and roll in potato chips. Place frozen sandwiches on a 13"x9" baking sheet. Bake at 325 degrees for 45 minutes. Serve with hot chicken gravy poured over sandwiches.

BBQ Chicken Calzones

**Janice Woods,** Northern Cambria, PA

# Pepperoni Pizza Burgers

If your family just loves pizza and burgers, this recipe will make for a great change at mealtime.

### Makes 6 servings

1-1/2 lbs. lean ground beef
1/2 lb. Italian ground pork sausage
1/2 t. Italian seasoning
12 slices mozzarella and/or provolone cheese
3-oz. pkg. sliced pepperoni
6 kaiser rolls, split
softened butter to taste
3/4 c. pizza sauce
grated Parmesan cheese to taste

In a large bowl, combine beef, sausage and seasoning. Mix well; form into 6 patties. Grill patties over medium heat to desired doneness, 3 to 4 minutes per side. When patties are nearly done, top each patty with 2 slices cheese and 5 to 6 slices pepperoni. Cover grill; continue cooking just until pepperoni is warmed through and cheese is melted. Spread cut sides of rolls with softened butter. Toast rolls on the grill until crisp and golden. Spread cut sides of rolls with sauce; sprinkle with Parmesan cheese. Serve burgers on buns.

★ FREEZE IT ★ To form hamburger patties in a flash, shape ground beef into a log and freeze it partially. Cut the log into slices, lay on a baking sheet and freeze until solid. Remove from baking sheets and place in freezer bags...perfect hamburgers when you're ready for them.

**Pepperoni Pizza Burgers**

**Sue Klapper,** Muskego, WI

# Romaine Chicken Caesar Wraps

We love this tasty sandwich! It's simple to fix...perfect when we all arrive home hungry for a quick bite.

### Makes 8 sandwiches

2 romaine lettuce hearts, chopped into bite-size pieces
2 c. cooked chicken, cubed
1 c. shredded Parmesan cheese
1/4 c. red onion, thinly sliced
1 c. creamy Caesar salad dressing
8 9-inch flavored or plain flour tortillas
Optional: additional salad dressing

Place lettuce in a large bowl. Add chicken, cheese, onion and salad dressing; toss well to coat and set aside. Soften tortillas in microwave oven, about 20 seconds on high. To make wraps, place each tortilla on a plate and spoon salad mixture along the center. Drizzle with additional dressing, if desired. Roll up tortilla from one side, burrito-style; fold the bottom up and in to hold the salad.

**Peggy Pelfrey,** Fort Riley, KS

# Greek Chicken Pitas

Top with crumbled feta cheese and sliced black olives...delicious!

### Makes 4 servings

1 onion, diced
3 cloves garlic, minced
1 lb. boneless, skinless chicken breasts, cut into strips
1 t. lemon-pepper seasoning
1/2 t. dried oregano
1/4 t. allspice
1/4 c. plain yogurt
1/4 c. sour cream
1/2 c. cucumber, peeled and diced
4 rounds pita bread, halved and split

Place onion and garlic in a 3 to 4-quart slow cooker; set aside. Sprinkle chicken with seasonings; place in slow cooker. Cover and cook on high setting for 4 to 5 hours or until chicken is no longer pink. Stir together yogurt, sour cream and cucumber in a small bowl; chill. Fill pita halves with chicken and drizzle with yogurt sauce.

Romaine Chicken Caesar Wraps

**Karen DeSantis,** Lockport, NY

# Dad's Wimpy Burgers

My father made these tasty burgers often at home. Many years ago, he was a cook at a Civilian Conservation Corps camp in Pennsylvania, where he often made them for his commander. Sadly, Dad has been gone since 1999, but he lives on in his recipes. I still make these burgers for my husband and son.

*Serves 6 to 8*

2 lbs. ground beef
1/2 c. catsup
1 egg, beaten
1 onion, chopped
1 t. salt
1 c. Italian-flavored dry bread crumbs
6 to 8 hamburger buns, split

In a large bowl, combine beef, catsup, egg, onion and salt; mix well. Form into 6 to 8 patties; flatten to desired thickness. Place bread crumbs in a shallow pan. Pat each side of patties in crumbs until coated. Place patties in a lightly greased 13"x9" baking pan. Bake, uncovered, at 350 degrees for 20 to 25 minutes, turning over after 8 minutes. Patties may also be pan-fried in a lightly greased skillet over medium heat. Cook on each side for 6 to 8 minutes, until lightly browned. Serve on buns.

★ FREEZE IT ★ Wrap up leftover dinner rolls and freeze, then grate while still frozen to use in any recipe that calls for bread crumbs.

Dad's Wimpy Burgers

**Kaylene Duncan,** Churubusco, IN

# Aloha Sandwiches

This sandwich couldn't be any easier to prepare...just toss together all the ingredients and serve!

### Serves 4 to 8

3 10-oz. cans chicken, drained
1 c. celery, chopped
1 c. seedless grapes, halved
1 c. mayonnaise-type salad dressing
1/2 c. chopped pecans
1/4 c. whipping cream
1 t. salt
12-oz. pkg. Hawaiian rolls, split

Combine all ingredients except salt and rolls; toss to mix well. Sprinkle with salt; blend well and spoon over rolls.

**Marie Benfield,** Clarkesville, GA

# Pulled BBQ Chicken Buns

This is a real go-to recipe...it's so easy. Everyone I have shared it with enjoys it as much as I do. Serve with coleslaw and chips!

### Makes 6 servings

4 to 6 boneless, skinless chicken
   breasts
1/2 c. water
3 T. white vinegar
3 T. Worcestershire sauce
1 t. ground cumin
favorite barbecue sauce to taste
6 sandwich buns, split

In a slow cooker, combine all ingredients except barbecue sauce and buns. Cover and cook on low setting for 6 to 8 hours, until chicken is tender. Drain off liquid. Shred chicken using 2 forks. Add desired amount of sauce; cover and cook another 30 minutes. Serve chicken on buns.

Aloha Sandwiches

**Geneva Rogers,** Gillette, WY

# Papa's Italian Sandwiches

A really tasty sandwich! Keep cooked sausages with sauce mixture separate from rolls and cheese, then assemble the sandwiches when you arrive at your picnic spot.

*Makes 24 sandwiches*

**24 Italian pork sausage links**
**5 green peppers, thinly sliced**
**1 onion, chopped**
**12-oz. can tomato paste**
**15-oz. can tomato sauce**
**1 c. water**
**1 T. sugar**
**5 cloves garlic, minced**
**1-1/4 t. dried oregano**
**1 t. dried basil**
**1 t. salt**
**24 hoagie rolls, split**
**Garnish: grated Parmesan cheese**

Brown 6 to 8 sausages at a time in a large Dutch oven over medium heat. Drain sausages and set aside, reserving 3 tablespoons drippings in Dutch oven. Add peppers and onion. Sauté until crisp-tender; drain. Stir in tomato paste, tomato sauce, water, sugar, garlic and seasonings. Add sausages; bring to a boil over medium heat. Reduce heat; simmer, covered, 30 to 45 minutes. Serve on rolls; sprinkle with cheese.

★ TAKE IT TO GO ★ Wrap Papa's Italian Sandwiches in aluminum foil and tuck into a basket with mini bags of potato chips, a couple of frosty sodas and a giant dill pickle from the deli...all you need for a tasty picnic!

Papa's Italian Sandwiches

**Teresa Willett,** Ontario, Canada

# Grilled Chicken & Zucchini Wraps

These wraps are a huge hit with my family...even my son who claims he doesn't like zucchini!

### Makes 8 servings

4 boneless, skinless chicken breasts
4 to 6 zucchini, sliced lengthwise into
   1/4-inch thick slices
1 to 2 T. olive oil
salt and pepper to taste
1/2 c. ranch salad dressing, divided
8  10-inch whole-grain flour tortillas
8 leaves lettuce
Garnish: shredded Cheddar cheese

Brush chicken and zucchini with olive oil; sprinkle with salt and pepper. Grill chicken over medium-high heat for 5 minutes. Turn chicken over; add zucchini to grill. Grill 5 minutes longer, or until chicken juices run clear and zucchini is tender. Slice chicken into strips; set aside. For each wrap, spread one tablespoon salad dressing on a tortilla. Top with a lettuce leaf, 1/2 cup chicken and 3 to 4 slices of zucchini. Sprinkle with cheese; roll up.

**Regina Kostyu,** Delaware, OH

# Shredded Beef Sandwiches

So good to have for company because you can spend time with them and not in the kitchen. It's also nice to come home to after being at a track meet or soccer game and have dinner ready.

### Serves 12 to 16

2 to 4-lb. boneless beef chuck roast
10-3/4 oz. can cream of mushroom
   soup
1-1/2 oz. pkg. onion soup mix
16 buns

Place roast in a slow cooker; spread mushroom soup over top and sprinkle with onion soup mix. Cover and cook on high setting for 4 to 6 hours. Shred and stir with a fork. Spoon onto buns.

**Grilled Chicken & Zucchini Wraps**

**Krista Marshall,** Fort Wayne, IN

# Beef & Bean Tostadas

Kids will love this crunchy eat-with-your-hands supper. Tostadas are like an open-faced taco...great for Mexican-themed parties!

### Makes 6 servings

1 lb. ground beef
1/2 c. onion, finely diced
1-1/4 oz. pkg. taco seasoning mix
1 c. water
15-oz. can nacho cheese sauce
15-oz. can refried beans
6 corn tostada shells
Garnish: pico de gallo or salsa

Brown beef and onion in a skillet over medium heat; drain. Add taco seasoning and water; cook, stirring occasionally, for 5 to 7 minutes, until thickened. Meanwhile, place cheese sauce and beans in separate microwave-safe bowls. Heat, stirring occasionally, until warmed through. Spread tostada shells evenly with beans; top each with about 1/4 cup beef mixture. Drizzle with cheese sauce; garnish with pico de gallo or salsa.

★ TIME-SAVING SHORTCUT ★ Are lots of kids coming for an after-game party? Make it easy with do-it-yourself tostadas...guests can add their own favorite toppings. Round out the menu with pitchers of soft drinks and a yummy dessert. Simple and fun!

Beef & Bean Tostadas

**Linda Campbell,** Huber Heights, OH

# Italian Meatloaf Sandwiches

This great flavor combo also works with leftover roast beef or pot roast.

*Makes 4 servings*

14-oz. French bread loaf
4 one-inch-thick cold meatloaf
    slices
1 c. marinara or spaghetti sauce
8-oz. pkg. shredded Italian cheese
    blend
1/4 t. dried Italian seasoning

Cut bread into fourths; cut quarters in half horizontally. Place bread quarters, cut sides up, on a baking sheet. Top each bread bottom with one meatloaf slice, 2 tablespoons marinara sauce and 1/4 cup cheese. Top each bread top with 2 tablespoons marinara sauce and 1/4 cup cheese; sprinkle with Italian seasoning. Bake at 375 degrees for 10 to 15 minutes or until cheese melts and meat is thoroughly heated. Top bread bottoms with bread tops and serve sandwiches immediately.

**Kisha Landeros,** Pacific, MO

# Hoagie Hamburger Boats

This is a dish my brother and I would always request! My mom made these sandwiches for us for busy afternoons and school nights. Simple to make, very filling and easy clean-up.

*Makes 6 servings*

6 hoagie rolls
1 to 1-1/2 lbs. ground beef
10-3/4 oz. can cream of
    mushroom soup
salt and pepper to taste
6 slices American cheese

Slice off the tops of hoagie rolls. Pull out the centers of rolls to create "boats." Set aside tops and bread pieces. In a skillet over medium heat, brown beef; drain. Stir in soup and bread pieces; season with salt and pepper. Simmer for a few minutes, until heated through. Place rolls on a baking sheet; spoon beef mixture into rolls. Add cheese slices; replace tops onto rolls. Bake at 400 degrees for 10 to 15 minutes, until cheese is melted.

Hoagie Hamburger Boats

**Jessica Johnson,** Boston, MA

# Game Day Stromboli

We like this when it's hot out of the oven and even enjoy it cold the next day for lunch.

### Makes 8 servings

2 loaves frozen bread dough
1/2 lb. deli baked ham, thinly sliced
1/2 lb. deli roast beef, thinly sliced
1/2 lb. deli bologna, thinly sliced
1/2 lb. Cheddar cheese, thinly sliced
1/2 c. red pepper, diced
1/2 c. onion, diced
1/4 c. sliced black olives
1/4 c. sliced green olives
1/2 t. garlic salt
1/2 t. Italian seasoning
2 T. olive oil

Line a 15"x10" jelly-roll pan with parchment paper; spray with non-stick vegetable spray. Place both frozen loaves end-to-end on pan; thaw according to package directions. When thawed, roll out both loaves together to cover the pan. Layer meats and cheese over dough; scatter red pepper, onion and olives over cheese. Sprinkle with seasonings. Roll up layered dough jelly-roll style, starting on one long edge; place seam-side down on pan. Let rise for one hour. Drizzle olive oil over rolled dough. Bake at 400 degrees for 15 minutes. Reduce oven temperature to 350 degrees; bake an additional 15 minutes. Slice and serve hot or cold.

★ TAKE IT TO GO ★ Host a casual outdoor lunch for family & friends...perfect for a sunny game day! Toss stadium blankets over tables and serve Game Day Stromboli, fresh fruit and your favorite potato salad. Bottles of soda can be kept cold in an ice-filled galvanized bucket. Fun!

Game Day Stromboli

**Maya Andrews,** San Francisco, CA

# Roast Beef Pinwheel Sandwiches

These sandwiches were my favorite when I was growing up. They are so easy to make. The tender roast beef paired with the melty cheese makes them so delicious!

*Makes 8 sandwiches*

8-oz. tube refrigerated crescent rolls
4 slices American cheese, each cut
   into 4 squares
8 square slices deli roast beef

Roll out crescent rolls; pinch seams together to create one large rectangle. Cut dough into 8 equal squares. On each dough square, place one small square of cheese in the center, followed by a slice of ham, then topped with another small square of cheese. Make a one-inch slice in each of the 4 corners of dough square, angled toward the center of the sandwich. Pull the piece of dough from the right side of each slice and fold it to the center of the sandwich, to look like a pinwheel. Fasten with a wooden toothpick, if desired. Place sandwiches on an ungreased baking sheet. Bake at 350 degrees for 10 to 15 minutes, until dough is golden and cheese is melted.

★ SIMPLE INGREDIENT SWAP ★
**This recipe is so easy to customize for family & friends! Try using deli ham and Cheddar cheese, or pastrami and Swiss.**

**Roast Beef Pinwheel Sandwiches**

**Cheryl Sullivan,** Winfield, IA

# French Dips on a Budget

One day, my mother and I were craving a French dip sandwich, so we put our heads together and came up with this tasty recipe.

### Serves 4 to 6

3 to 4-lb. beef rump roast
1/2 c. soy sauce
1.35-oz. pkg. onion soup mix
salt and pepper to taste
3 to 4 c. water
4 to 6 sandwich rolls, split

Place roast in a slow cooker. Drizzle with soy sauce; sprinkle with soup mix, salt and pepper. Add enough water to cover roast. Cover and cook on low setting for 9 to 10 hours, until beef is very tender. Remove beef from slow cooker and slice or shred. To serve, place beef on rolls for sandwiches; serve with juices from slow cooker for dipping.

**Cris Goode,** Mooresville, IN

# Momma's Quick Meatball Subs

We love our local sub shop's French bread. We often buy day-old loaves for a delicious way to dress up this yummy family treat.

### Makes 4 servings

1 lb. extra-lean ground beef
20 saltine crackers, crushed
12-oz. bottle chili sauce, divided
1/4 c. grated Parmesan cheese
2 egg whites, beaten
salt and pepper to taste
15-oz. jar pizza sauce, warmed
2 loaves French baguettes, halved
   and split
2 cups favorite shredded cheese

Combine beef, cracker crumbs, half of chili sauce, Parmesan cheese, egg whites, salt and pepper in a bowl. Mix well; form into 16 (1-1/2 inch) meatballs. Place on a baking sheet sprayed with non-stick vegetable spray. Bake at 400 degrees for 15 minutes, or until golden, turning meatballs halfway through. Add baked meatballs to warmed sauce. Fill each half-loaf with 4 meatballs and sprinkle with cheese. Serve with remaining chili sauce on the side.

French Dips on a Budget

**Valerie Gardner,** Lyman, SC

# Grilled Flank Steak Sandwich

On a hot summer's evening, it's nice to keep the kitchen cool! Grill the steak in the backyard, then finish the sandwich indoors.

### *Serves 4 to 6*

1 to 1-1/2 lb. beef flank steak
seasoned salt and pepper to taste
1 sweet onion, thinly sliced
1 green or red pepper, thinly sliced
2 to 3 t. olive oil
mayonnaise to taste
8 to 12 slices country-style bread
4 to 6 slices provolone cheese
softened butter to taste

Grill steak over medium heat to desired doneness. Remove from grill; add seasonings and let rest for about 10 minutes. Slice steak slice thinly on the diagonal. Meanwhile, in a skillet over medium-high heat, sauté onion and pepper in oil until onion is caramelized, about 10 minutes. Spread mayonnaise on one side of bread. Assemble sandwiches with bread, sliced steak, onion mixture and cheese slices. Spread a little butter over outside of sandwiches. Heat a countertop grill, panini press or grill pan. Grill sandwiches until toasted and cheese is melted.

★ HOT TIP ★ Ask everyone to a soup & sandwich party...especially inviting in chilly weather! With a big pot of your heartiest soup simmering on the stove, freshly made Grilled Flank Steak Sandwiches and warm fruit cobbler for dessert, everyone will be happy and satisfied...especially the hostess!

Grilled Flank Steak Sandwich

**Soren Drier,** Columbus, OH

# Waffle Iron Grilled Beef & Cheese

You'll love the gooey cheese and the dimples from the waffle iron! Add a bowl of hot soup and you have a quick busy-day meal.

### Makes 1 sandwich

1 T. butter, softened
2 slices sandwich bread
3/4 c. shredded fontina, Muenster
　or Cheddar cheese
2 slices deli roast beef

Spread butter over one side of each bread slice. Place one bread slice on a heated waffle iron, butter-side down. Top with cheese, roast beef and second bread slice, butter-side up. Close waffle iron; cook for about 2 minutes, until golden.

**Angie Stone,** Argillite, KY

# Kentucky Hot Browns

I learned to make these cheesy-good sandwiches when I was very young. They're a real favorite here in Kentucky.

### Makes 6 servings

1/4 c. butter
1/4 c. all-purpose flour
2 c. milk
2 cubes chicken bouillon
16-oz. pkg. pasteurized
　cheese spread, cubed
6 slices bread, toasted
12 slices deli turkey
6 slices deli ham
6 slices bacon, crisply cooked
6 slices tomato

Melt butter in a heavy saucepan over low heat. Stir in flour until smooth. Cook one minute, stirring constantly. Stir in milk and bouillon cubes. Cook until thick and bubbly. Add cheese and stir until smooth. Place toast slices in a buttered 13"x9" baking pan. Layer each with turkey and ham. Evenly spread cheese sauce over ham. Top each with bacon and tomato. Bake, uncovered, at 350 degrees for 3 to 5 minutes, until bubbly.

**Waffle Iron Grilled Beef & Cheese**

**Sandy Carpenter,** Washington, WV

# Scrumptious Chicken Sandwiches

These taste so much like a popular restaurant's sandwiches but cost much less!

*Serves 8 to 10*

1 egg, beaten
1 c. milk
4 to 6 boneless, skinless chicken
   breasts
1 c. all-purpose flour
2-1/2 T. powdered sugar
1 T. kosher salt
1/2 t. pepper
Optional: 1/8 t. allspice
oil for frying
4 to 6 hamburger buns, split and
   lightly toasted
Garnish: mayonnaise, dill pickle
   slices

Mix egg and milk together in an 11"x7" baking pan. Place chicken in pan, turn to coat and refrigerate for one hour. In a bowl, combine flour, sugar and spices. In a heavy skillet, heat one inch of oil to 400 degrees. Working in batches of 3, drain chicken, reserving egg mixture, and lightly dredge in flour mixture. Dip back into egg mixture, then into flour mixture again. Place very carefully into hot oil. Fry for 8 to 10 minutes, until done on both sides and juices run clear. Drain chicken on a wire rack. Assemble sandwiches on toasted buns and garnish as desired.

★ HOT TIP ★ Grandma's good old cast-iron skillet is wonderful for frying chicken. If the skillet hasn't been used in awhile, season it first...rub it all over with oil, bake at 300 degrees for an hour and let it cool completely in the oven.

Scrumptious Chicken Sandwiches

**Tori Willis,** Champaign, IL

# Yiayia's Chicken Pitas

Though not exactly like my grandma's famous Greek sandwiches, they're pretty darn close!

### Makes 4 servings

1/2 c. plain yogurt
1/4 c. cucumber, finely chopped
1/2 t. dill weed
1/4 t. dried mint, crushed
4 pita bread rounds
4 lettuce leaves
2 c. cooked chicken, cubed
1 tomato, thinly sliced
1/3 c. crumbled feta cheese

In a small bowl, stir together yogurt, cucumber, dill weed and mint; set aside. For each sandwich, layer a pita with lettuce, chicken, tomato and cheese. Spoon yogurt mixture on top. Roll up pita and secure with a wooden toothpick. Serve immediately.

**JoAnn,** Gooseberry Patch

# Cobb Salad Subs

A clever twist on an old favorite.

### Makes 4 sandwiches

1-1/3 c. cooked chicken, diced
2 roma tomatoes, diced
4 slices bacon, crisply cooked and crumbled
1/2 c. crumbled blue cheese
2 eggs, hard-boiled, peeled and diced
4 submarine buns, split and toasted
4 leaves lettuce

Combine all ingredients except buns and lettuce. Drizzle with Avocado Dressing and toss to coat. Spoon mixture over bottom halves of buns; add lettuce leaves and top halves of buns.

### Avocado Dressing:

3 T. olive oil
1 T. white wine vinegar
1 t. Dijon mustard
1/2 t. salt
1/2 t. pepper
1 avocado, pitted, peeled and diced

Combine all ingredients except avocado; whisk until well blended. Stir in avocado.

Yiayia's Chicken Pitas

**Janice Henderson,** Columbus, OH

# Dilly Chicken Sandwiches

This is a great sandwich for a family get-together. Bread & butter pickles make it taste even better!

### Makes 4 servings

4 boneless, skinless chicken breasts
6 T. butter, softened and divided
1 clove garlic, minced
3/4 t. dill weed, divided
8 slices French bread
4 T. cream cheese, softened
2 t. lemon juice
Garnish: lettuce leaves, tomato
  slices, bread & butter pickles

Place chicken breasts between 2 pieces of wax paper. Using a mallet, flatten to 1/4-inch thickness; set aside. On a cast-iron griddle over medium-high heat, melt 3 tablespoons butter; stir in garlic and 1/2 teaspoon dill weed. Add chicken; cook on both sides until juices run clear. Remove and keep warm. Spread both sides of bread with remaining butter. Wipe griddle clean. Over medium heat, grill bread on both sides until golden. Combine remaining dill weed, cream cheese and lemon juice. Spread on one side of 4 slices grilled bread. Top with chicken; garnish as desired. Top with remaining bread.

---

★ DOUBLE DUTY ★ If you bought a bunch of fresh herbs for a recipe that calls for just a couple of teaspoons, chop the extra herbs and add to a tossed salad. Fresh parsley, mint, dill, chives and basil all add zest.

---

**Dilly Chicken Sandwiches**

**Jo Ann,** Gooseberry Patch

# Rosemary-Dijon Chicken Croissants

Pair with fruit salad cups and sweet tea for a delightful brunch.

*Makes 10 mini sandwiches*

3 c. cooked chicken breast, chopped
1/3 c. green onion, chopped
1/4 c. smoked almonds, chopped
1/4 c. plain yogurt
1/4 c. mayonnaise
1 t. fresh rosemary, chopped
1 t. Dijon mustard
1/8 t. salt
1/8 t. pepper
10 mini croissants, split
Garnish: leaf lettuce

Combine all ingredients except bread and lettuce, mixing well. Arrange lettuce leaves inside croissants; spread with chicken mixture.

**Jamie Davis,** Fremont, CA

# Chicken-Cheddar Wraps

This is a great way to use leftover chicken...it'll become a family favorite.

*Makes 12 sevings*

1 c. sour cream
1 c. salsa
2 T. mayonnaise
4 c. cooked chicken, cubed
2 c. shredded Cheddar cheese
1 c. sliced mushrooms
2 c. lettuce, shredded
12 flour tortillas
1 c. guacamole
Garnish: tomato wedges

Combine sour cream, salsa and mayonnaise; add chicken, cheese and mushrooms. Divide lettuce between tortillas; top with 1/4 cup chicken mixture on each tortilla. Spread with guacamole; roll up tortilla. Place tortillas on serving dish; garnish with any remaining guacamole and tomato wedges.

Rosemary-Dijon Chicken Croissants

**Lisa Sanders,** Shoals, IN

# Barbecue Steak Sandwiches

A great party recipe! Roll up leftovers in tortillas for a fast lunch.

### Serves 12 to 14

3 lbs. boneless beef round steak,
   cut into several large pieces
2 onions, chopped
3/4 c. celery, thinly sliced
1/2 c. catsup
1/2 to 3/4 c. water
1/3 c. lemon juice
1/3 c. Worcestershire sauce
3 T. brown sugar, packed
3 T. cider vinegar
2 t. mustard
2 t. salt
1 t. pepper
1 t. chili powder
1/2 t. paprika
1/2 t. hot pepper sauce
12 to 14 sandwich buns, split

Place steak, onions and celery in a slow cooker; set aside. Combine remaining ingredients except buns in a bowl; stir and pour over steak mixture. Cover and cook on low setting for 6 to 8 hours, until steak is tender. Remove steak and cool slightly; shred with a fork and return to sauce in slow cooker. Heat through and serve on buns.

★ TIME-SAVING SHORTCUT ★ Jump-start tomorrow's dinner! Chop and assemble ingredients tonight, refrigerating meat and veggies in separate containers. In the morning, toss everything in the slow cooker...you're set to go!

**Barbecue Steak Sandwiches**

**Barbara Cooper,** Orion, IL

# Pulled Chicken & Slaw Sandwiches

These sandwiches are super easy because you start with a roasted chicken from the deli. The creamy slaw adds a nice crunch...yum!

### Makes 6 sandwiches

1 c. favorite barbecue sauce
1 c. catsup
1/2 c. water
1 t. lemon juice
2/3 c. brown sugar, packed
1 deli roast chicken, boned and
    shredded
6 buns, split
Garnish: deli coleslaw

In a large saucepan, combine barbecue sauce, catsup, water, lemon juice and brown sugar. Stir well; add chicken. Cook over medium heat until mixture is heated through. Serve on buns; spoon slaw over chicken.

**Barbara Etzweiler,** Millersburg, PA

# Chicken Burgers

A yummy twist on traditional hamburgers!

### Makes 4 to 6 sandwiches

1 lb. ground chicken
1 onion, chopped
1/8 t. garlic powder
1/4 c. fresh bread crumbs
3 T. chicken broth
1 t. Dijon mustard
1 t. salt-free vegetable seasoning
    salt
pepper to taste
4 to 6 hamburger buns

Combine all ingredients, except hamburger buns, in a large mixing bowl. Stir lightly with a fork until well blended. Shape into 4 to 6 burgers. Heat an iron skillet and spray with non-stick vegetable spray. Brown chicken burgers until cooked throughout and nicely browned. Serve on buns.

Pulled Chicken & Slaw Sandwiches

Chicken & Sausage Skilletini, Page 218

# CHAPTER FOUR

# Dinners

**Sensational Sirloin Kabobs, Page 224**  **Deep-Dish Pizza, Page 246**

**Michael Anderson,** New Orleans, LA

# Festive Cajun Pepper Steak

Cajun seasoning kicks up the flavor of saucy beef sirloin tips spooned over yummy mashed potatoes.

*Serves 4 to 6*

1-1/2 lbs. beef sirloin tips
1 t. salt-free Cajun seasoning
1 T. oil
1 green pepper, chopped
1 onion, chopped
3 cloves garlic, minced
14-1/2 oz. can diced tomatoes
14-1/2 oz. can beef broth
2 t. Worcestershire sauce
1 t. white wine vinegar
1/2 t. dried basil
1/4 t. salt
1/8 t. pepper
2 T. cornstarch
2 T. cold water
22-oz. pkg. refrigerated or frozen
    mashed potatoes

Sprinkle beef tips with Cajun seasoning. In a large skillet over medium-high heat, cook beef in oil for 10 minutes, or until browned. Drain. Add green pepper, onion and garlic; sauté for 3 minutes. Stir in tomatoes with juice, beef broth, Worcestershire sauce, vinegar and seasonings. Bring to a boil; reduce heat to medium-low. Cover and simmer for one hour, or until beef is tender, stirring occasionally. Stir together cornstarch and water until smooth; stir into beef mixture. Bring to a boil; cook and stir for 2 minutes, or until thickened. Heat mashed potatoes according to package directions; serve beef mixture over potatoes.

★ SIMPLE INGREDIENT SWAP ★
**Fresh herbs give a wonderful flavor boost to foods! For one teaspoon of a dried herb like dill or rosemary, simply substitute one tablespoon of the fresh herb.**

Festive Cajun Pepper Steak

Cathy Gearheart, Narrows, VA

# Amanda's Chicken & Orzo

A great meal in about 20 minutes. This was a staple when my daughter was involved in sports and needed a light, quick, nutritious meal before a game.

### Makes 4 servings

4 boneless, skinless chicken breasts
1 t. dried basil
salt and pepper to taste
4 T. olive oil, divided
2 zucchini, sliced
8-oz. pkg. orzo pasta, uncooked
1 T. butter, softened
2 T. red wine vinegar
Optional: 1 t. fresh dill, snipped
Garnish: lemon wedges

Sprinkle chicken with basil, salt and pepper. Heat 2 tablespoons oil in a skillet over medium heat. Add chicken to skillet and cook, turning once, for 12 minutes, or until juices run clear. Remove chicken to a plate and keep warm. Add zucchini to skillet and cook for 3 minutes, or until crisp-tender. Meanwhile, cook orzo according to package directions; drain and stir in butter. Whisk together remaining oil, vinegar and dill, if using; drizzle over orzo and toss to mix. Season with additional salt and pepper, if desired. Serve chicken and zucchini with orzo, garnished with lemon wedges.

★ SIMPLE INGREDIENT SWAP ★
**Fresh herbs give a wonderful flavor boost to foods! For one teaspoon of a dried herb like dill or rosemary, simply substitute one tablespoon of the fresh herb.**

Amanda's Chicken & Orzo

**Liz Plotnick-Snay,** Gooseberry Patch

# Chicken & Snow Pea Stir-Fry

My husband and I are always looking for new chicken dishes. This recipe turned out delicious, especially with our own additions to it.

### Serves 3 to 4

1 T. reduced-sodium soy sauce
1 t. chile-garlic or curry sauce
1 T. rice vinegar
2 t. toasted sesame oil
1/2 lb. boneless, skinless chicken
   breast, cubed
1 T. fresh ginger, peeled and minced
3 c. snow peas, trimmed
3 green onions, chopped
3 T. unsalted cashews, broken
cooked rice
Optional: additional chile-garlic
   sauce

Combine sauces and vinegar in a small bowl; set aside. Heat oil in a skillet over medium-high heat. Add chicken; cook and stir until no longer pink in the center. Add ginger; cook and stir for about 30 seconds. Add snow peas and onions; cook until snow peas are just tender, about 2 to 4 minutes. Add soy sauce mixture; stir to coat well. Stir in cashews just before serving. Serve over cooked rice; top with more chile-garlic sauce, if desired.

★ FREEZE IT ★ Freezing cooked rice makes for quick-fix meals later. Use it for stir-fry dishes, to make soups thick and hearty, or mix in fresh vegetables for an easy side dish. Just freeze servings flat in plastic zipping bags. How clever!

Chicken & Snow Pea Stir-Fry

**Carla Slajchert,** Saint Petersburg, FL

# Mom's Cola Chicken

Growing up, we knew Mom would be making this delicious, tender chicken whenever we saw her getting out the electric skillet.

### Makes 4 servings

1 to 2 T. oil
1-1/2 lbs. boneless, skinless chicken breasts
salt and pepper to taste
20-oz. bottle cola, divided
1 to 2 c. catsup, divided

Heat oil in a large skillet over medium heat. Add chicken to oil; sprinkle with salt and pepper and brown on both sides. Pour enough cola into skillet to cover chicken. Slowly add enough catsup to skillet until mixture reaches desired thicknesss. Cover and cook over medium heat for about 45 minutes, adding remaining cola and catsup, a little at a time, every 10 to 15 minutes, until chicken juices run clear.

**Stacy Lane,** Millsboro, DE

# Chicken Lo Mein

I first learned this recipe in my home economics class in high school. I took it home, revamped it a little, and we've been enjoying for over ten years now! You can use any meat and vegetables you have on hand. I often share the recipe with first-time cooks and newlyweds, since it's so easy to make and easy on the budget.

### Makes 5 servings

1 T. oil
2 boneless, skinless chicken breasts, sliced
1 to 2 c. chopped broccoli, carrots, cabbage, celery and/or mushrooms
4  3-oz. pkgs. low-sodium chicken-flavored ramen noodles
4 c. water
1 T. low-sodium soy sauce
2 t. cornstarch
1 t. garlic powder
1 t. dried parsley
Optional: onion powder to taste

Heat oil in a large saucepan over medium heat. Add chicken; sauté until golden. Add vegetables to saucepan; break up ramen noodles and add to saucepan. In a separate saucepan, bring water to a boil. Stir in remaining ingredients, adding contents of seasoning packets to taste; add to chicken mixture. Cover and cook over medium-high heat for about 10 minutes, until vegetables are tender.

Mom's Cola Chicken

**Mary Rose Kulczak,** Noblesville, IN

# Easy Chicken & Couscous

Starting with a deli roast chicken makes this dish super easy! Cooking the vegetables in the pot with the couscous also saves time and makes clean-up a breeze.

### Serves 4 to 6

1-1/4 c. water
4 T. olive oil, divided
5.8-oz. pkg. chicken-flavored couscous, uncooked
1/2 c. red pepper, chopped
3 T. onion, chopped
2 cloves garlic, minced
2 c. cooked chicken, cubed
6-oz. jar marinated artichoke hearts, drained and chopped
3.8-oz. can sliced black olives, drained
4-oz. container crumbled feta cheese

In a saucepan over high heat, bring water and 2 tablespoons oil to a boil; add seasoning packet from couscous package, red pepper, onion and garlic. Boil for 2 to 3 minutes. Add couscous and cook according to package directions. Remove from heat; cover and let stand for 5 minutes, until all liquid is absorbed. Fluff with a fork. In a large serving bowl, toss chicken, artichokes and olives. Stir in couscous mixture. Add remaining oil; mix well. Sprinkle with cheese.

**Easy Chicken & Couscous**

**Jack Johnson,** Kansas City, MO

# Dixie Fried Chicken

Fried chicken is comfort food at its best! And this crispy Southern-style chicken, complete with a creamy gravy, doesn't disappoint.

*Makes 4 servings*

**2-1/2 to 3-lb. broiler-fryer, cut up,
    or 2-1/2 lbs. assorted chicken pieces**
**1/2 t. salt**
**1/2 t. pepper**
**1-1/2 c. all-purpose flour**
**1 t. cayenne pepper**
**1 egg, lightly beaten**
**1/3 c. milk**
**oil for frying**

Season chicken with salt and pepper; set aside. Combine flour and cayenne pepper in a shallow dish; combine egg and milk in a separate dish. Dip chicken into egg mixture and dredge in flour mixture, coating chicken well. Pour oil to a depth of one inch in a heavy 10" to 12" skillet; heat oil to 350 degrees. Fry chicken in hot oil over medium heat for 15 to 20 minutes, until golden, turning occasionally. Remove smaller pieces earlier, if necessary, to prevent overbrowning. Drain chicken on paper towels, reserving 1/4 cup drippings in skillet for Cream Gravy. Serve with gravy.

*Cream Gravy:*

**1/4 c. reserved pan drippings**
**1/4 c. all-purpose flour**
**2-1/2 to 3 c. hot milk**
**1/2 t. salt**
**1/4 t. pepper**
**1/8 t. cayenne pepper**

Heat pan drippings in skillet over medium heat. Add flour, stirring until browned. Gradually add hot milk; cook, stirring constantly, until thick and bubbly. Stir in seasonings. Serve hot. Makes 2-3/4 cups.

Dixie Fried Chicken

**Judy Davis,** Muskogee, OK

# Mushroom-Garlic-Chicken Pizza

This recipe gets a big "YUM" at our house...try it! It's a great way to use leftover baked or grilled chicken too.

### Serves 6 to 8

12-inch Italian pizza crust
3/4 c. ranch salad dressing
2 T. garlic, minced
1 chicken breast, cooked and sliced
2 4-oz. cans sliced mushrooms, drained
salt and pepper to taste
8-oz. pkg. shredded mozzarella cheese
Optional: fresh oregano leaves, red pepper flakes

Place crust on an ungreased pizza pan or baking sheet. Spread salad dressing and garlic over crust. Arrange sliced chicken and mushrooms on top. Add salt and pepper to taste; cover with cheese. Bake at 400 degrees for 8 to 10 minutes, until cheese melts. Cut into wedges. Garnish with oregano and red pepper, if desired.

**Barbara Bower,** Orrville, OH

# Easy-As-1-2-3 Chicken Bake

Serve with steamed broccoli or asparagus.

### Makes 8 servings

3/4 c. corn flake cereal, crushed
3/4 c. grated Parmesan cheese
1-oz. pkg. Italian salad dressing mix
8 boneless, skinless chicken breasts
1/3 c. butter, melted

Mix cereal, Parmesan cheese and salad dressing mix together; coat chicken. Place in a single layer in a greased 13"x9" baking pan. Sprinkle remaining crumbs on top; drizzle with butter. Bake at 350 degrees for 45 minutes or until juices run clear when chicken is pierced with a fork.

Mushroom-Garlic-Chicken Pizza

**Emily Hartzell,** Portland, IN

# Hawaiian Chicken Kabobs

Light the tiki torches! This is the perfect recipe for grilling out with family & friends on a balmy summer night.

### Makes 6 servings

15-1/4 oz. can pineapple chunks in juice, drained and 1/2 c. juice reserved
1-1/2 lbs. boneless, skinless chicken breasts, cut into 1-inch cubes
1 lb. bacon, each slice cut into thirds
1 red or green pepper, cut into 1-inch squares
12 mushrooms
18 cherry tomatoes
6 skewers
cooked rice

Prepare Marinade, using reserved pineapple juice; refrigerate pineapple chunks. Place chicken in a large shallow glass dish. Pour marinade over chicken; cover and chill for at least one hour. Drain, pouring marinade into a small saucepan; bring to a boil for 3 minutes. Wrap each chicken cube in a piece of bacon. Thread ingredients onto skewers, alternating chicken, pineapple and vegetables. Grill skewers over medium to medium-high heat for 10 to 15 minutes, brushing often with marinade, until chicken juices run clear. Serve skewers over cooked rice.

### Marinade:

reserved 1/2 c. pineapple juice
1/2 c. soy sauce
1/4 c. canola oil
1 T. brown sugar, packed
2 t. ground ginger
1 t. garlic powder
1 t. dry mustard
1/4 t. pepper

In a small saucepan, stir together all ingredients. Bring to a boil over medium heat; reduce heat and simmer for 5 minutes. Cool slightly.

Hawaiian Chicken Kabobs

**Jewel Sharpe,** Raleigh, NC

# Tangy BBQ Chicken

Coffee lovers will like this chicken grilled with a coffee-based sauce. The recipe makes about 1-1/2 cups of the sauce...it's tasty on beef and pork as well as chicken.

*Makes 8 servings*

1 c. brewed coffee
1 c. catsup
1/2 c. sugar
1/2 c. Worcestershire sauce
1/4 c. cider vinegar
1/8 t. pepper
8 chicken thighs and drumsticks

In a saucepan, combine all ingredients except chicken. Bring to a boil over medium heat; reduce heat to low. Simmer, uncovered, for 30 to 35 minutes until thickened, stirring occasionally. Grill chicken as desired, brushing with sauce as it cooks.

**Kathy Courington,** Canton, GA

# Simple Ginger Chicken

My daughter's girlfriend says this is the best chicken she has ever had. A friend shared the recipe with me years ago... every time I serve it, it disappears! It really is that simple and that good.

*Makes 8 servings*

6 to 8 chicken thighs
1/2 to 1 onion, chopped
1 c. low-sodium soy sauce
1 c. water
3 T. ground ginger, or to taste
cooked rice

Combine all ingredients except rice in a Dutch oven. Bring to a boil over medium-high heat; reduce heat to low. Cover and simmer for one hour, or until chicken juices run clear. Check occasionally, adding more water as needed. May also be cooked in a slow cooker on low setting for 6 to 8 hours. Serve over cooked rice.

**Tangy BBQ Chicken**

**Jennifer Smith,** Manchester, CT

# Chicken & Spinach Calzones

A great recipe using prepared dough...what a time-saver!

### Makes 4 servings

2 boneless, skinless chicken
   breasts, cubed
1 T. oil
1/4 c. onion, chopped
1 c. frozen chopped spinach, cooked
   and drained
2 t. dried basil
3/4 c. pizza sauce
1/2 c. ricotta cheese
3 oz. mozzarella cheese, cubed
11-oz. can refrigerated pizza dough

In a large skillet over medium-high heat, sauté chicken in oil until juices run clear when chicken is pierced with a fork. Add onion and sauté 2 minutes. Reduce heat to medium-low; add spinach, basil, pizza sauce and ricotta cheese. Remove from heat; stir in mozzarella cheese and set aside. Divide pizza dough into 4 equal pieces; roll each piece into a 6-inch circle. Divide chicken mixture among dough circles; fold dough in half. Seal edges with a fork; set on a lightly greased baking sheet. Bake at 425 degrees for 15 minutes, or until crust is golden.

Chicken & Spinach Calzones

Linda Strausburg, Arroyo Grande, CA

# Bacon-Wrapped Chicken

Any flavor cream cheese works in this recipe...use what you have on hand!

### Makes 2 servings

2 boneless, skinless chicken breasts,
   flattened to 1/2-inch thickness
1/2 t. salt
1/4 t. pepper
2 T. chive & onion cream cheese,
   softened and divided
2 T. chilled butter, divided
1/2 t. dried tarragon, divided
2 slices bacon

Sprinkle chicken with salt and pepper. Spread one tablespoon cream cheese over each chicken breast; top with one tablespoon butter and 1 /4 teaspoon tarragon. Roll up and wrap with one slice bacon; secure with a toothpick. Place chicken seam-side down on an ungreased baking sheet. Bake at 400 degrees for 30 minutes, or until juices run clear when chicken is pierced with a fork. Increase temperature to broil; broil 8 to 10 minutes, until bacon is crisp.

Shirley Howie, Foxboro, MA

# Easy Chicken & Tomato Rice

This recipes comes together so quickly. It's perfect for busy nights.

### Makes 2 servings

10-1/2 oz. can chicken broth
14-1/2 oz. can stewed tomatoes
1 t. garlic powder
1 t. dried basil
2 c. cooked chicken, cubed
1-1/2 c. instant rice, uncooked
1 c. peas

In a saucepan over high heat, combine broth, tomatoes with juice and seasonings. Bring to a boil. Add chicken, uncooked rice and peas; return to a boil. Remove from heat. Cover and let stand for 5 minutes, or until most of the liquid is absorbed. Fluff rice with a fork before serving.

Bacon-Wrapped Chicken

**Becky Holsinger,** Belpre, OH

# Easy Chicken Manicotti

Although I love to cook, I don't claim to be all that great at it. I was given this recipe when I got married and not only is it easy, it tastes great! I know when I make this dish it will be good, no matter what.

*Serves 5 to 7*

**26-oz. jar pasta sauce**
**1/2 c. water**
**10 boneless, skinless chicken tenders**
**1 t. garlic salt**
**1/2 t. Italian seasoning**
**10 manicotti pasta shells, uncooked**
**8-oz. pkg. shredded mozzarella cheese**
**Optional: chopped fresh basil and**
**oregano**

In a bowl, mix pasta sauce and water. Spread 1/3 of sauce mixture in an ungreased 13"x9" glass baking pan; set aside. Sprinkle chicken with seasonings. Insert one chicken tender into each uncooked manicotti shell, stuffing from each end, if necessary. Arrange shells over sauce mixture in baking pan. Pour remaining sauce mixture evenly over shells, covering completely. Cover with aluminum foil. Bake at 350 degrees for about one hour, until shells are tender and chicken is no longer pink in the center. Top with cheese. Bake, uncovered, for 5 minutes, or until cheese is melted. Garnish with herbs, if desired.

**Easy Chicken Manicotti**

**Heather Webb,** Richmond, VA

# Oven Chicken Cordon Bleu

Pecans lend a crunchy touch to this favorite.

### Makes 4 servings

4 boneless, skinless chicken breasts
4 t. Dijon mustard, divided
1 t. garlic, minced and divided
4 slices deli baked ham
4 slices Swiss cheese
4 t. olive oil
1 c. chopped pecans

Flatten chicken breasts to 1/2-inch thickness using the flat side of a meat mallet or rolling pin. Top each piece with one teaspoon mustard and 1/4 teaspoon garlic. Place one slice ham and one slice cheese on each piece; roll up and secure with toothpicks. Brush oil over rolls; dredge in pecans. Place in a greased 13"x9" baking pan. Bake, uncovered, at 350 degrees for 35 to 40 minutes, until chicken juices run clear.

**Nancy Kailihiwa,** Wheatland, CA

# Hidden Spinach Meatloaf

I started making this meatloaf in an effort to get my kids to eat more vegetables. They used to call the spinach my "special seasoning." Years later, the kids found out what it was, but they still love it for our Sunday supper.

### Makes 2 meatloaves; each serves 6

10-3/4 oz. can tomato soup
5 to 10 dashes hot pepper sauce
2 lbs. lean ground beef
1/2 c. onion, finely chopped
10-oz. pkg. frozen chopped spinach, thawed and well-drained
1/2 c. dry bread crumbs
1/2 c. grated Parmesan cheese
1/2 c. shredded Mozzarella cheese
2 eggs, beaten
1 T. Worcestershire sauce
1 t. salt
1/2 t. pepper

In a bowl, combine soup and hot sauce; mix well. Remove 1/2 cup of soup mixture to a large bowl and set the rest aside. Add remaining ingredients to large bowl. Mix well and form into 2 loaves; place in 2 well-greased 9"x5" loaf pans. Bake, uncovered, at 350 degrees for 45 minutes to one hour, until no longer pink in the center. Microwave remaining soup mixture for one minute, or until hot; spread over meatloaves. Second meatloaf may be frozen.

**Oven Chicken Cordon Bleu**

**Kendall Hale,** Lynn, MA

# Roast Chicken Dijon

This recipe is so simple and scrumptious...we love it! Sometimes I'll make extra sauce to toss with redskin potatoes and tuck them around the chicken for a meal-in-one.

*Serves 4 to 6*

3 to 4-lb. roasting chicken
1/4 c. Dijon mustard
2 T. lemon juice
1 T. olive oil
salt and pepper to taste

Place chicken on a rack in an ungreased roasting pan. Mix mustard, lemon juice and oil in a small bowl. Brush mixture over chicken; sprinkle with salt and pepper. Bake, uncovered, at 425 degrees for 40 to 55 minutes, until juices run clear when chicken is pierced with a fork. Let stand for several minutes before slicing.

★ TIME-SAVING SHORTCUT ★
Get a head start on dinner by peeling and cutting up potatoes the night before. They won't turn dark if you cover them with water before refrigerating them.

Roast Chicken Dijon

**Mary Kelly,** Jefferson City, MO

# Chicken & Rotini Stir-Fry

This very tasty, light recipe is so easy to make. You're gonna love it!

*Serves 4 to 6*

2-1/2 c. rotini pasta, uncooked
2 T. olive oil
2 boneless, skinless chicken breasts,
    cut into strips
1 c. broccoli flowerets
1 c. carrots, peeled and cut into curls
    with a vegetable peeler
1/2 c. red onion, sliced
1/4 c. water
1/2 t. chicken bouillon granules
1/2 t. fresh tarragon, snipped
2 T. grated Parmesan cheese

Cook pasta according to package directions; drain. Meanwhile, heat oil in a large skillet over medium-high heat. Add chicken, broccoli, carrots and onion. Cook and stir until broccoli is crisp-tender, about 10 minutes. Add water, bouillon and tarragon; cook and stir until juices run clear when chicken is pierced. Add pasta and cheese. Toss to coat; serve immediately.

**Diana Chaney,** Olathe, KS

# Broccoli Beef Stir-Fry

My son likes the taste of Chinese pepper steak, but won't eat the green peppers. Now I make it with broccoli instead, and he's joined the clean plate club!

*Makes 4 servings*

.87-oz. pkg. brown gravy mix
1 c. water
1/4 t. pepper
1 T. oil
3/4 to 1 lb. beef flank steak, sliced into
    thin strips
2 c. broccoli, cut into bite-size
    flowerets
cooked rice or linguine pasta
Optional: soy sauce

Whisk together gravy mix, water and pepper in a bowl; set aside. Heat oil in a large skillet over medium-high heat. Add beef strips; cook and stir for 3 to 4 minutes. Stir in broccoli and gravy; bring to a boil. Reduce heat to low; cover and simmer 5 to 8 minutes, or until broccoli is crisp-tender. Serve over cooked rice or pasta, with soy sauce if desired.

Chicken & Rotini Stir-Fry

Elizabeth Cisneros, Chino Hills, CA

# Chicken & Sausage Skilletini

I like to serve this hearty one-pan dish with French bread and olive oil for dipping.

### Serves 4 to 6

1/4 c. olive oil
2 boneless, skinless chicken
   breasts, cubed
1/2 lb. spicy ground pork sausage
1 red onion, thinly sliced
2 cloves garlic, minced
14-1/2 oz. can diced tomatoes
1 red pepper, sliced
3 T. brown sugar, packed
1 t. dried basil
1/2 t. dried oregano
1/8 t. salt
1/8 t. pepper
16-oz. pkg. linguine pasta, cooked
Optional: fresh oregano leaves

Heat oil in a large skillet over medium heat. Add chicken, sausage, onion and garlic; cook until juices run clear when chicken is pierced. Add tomatoes with juice, red pepper, brown sugar and seasonings; simmer for 5 minutes. Add cooked pasta and simmer an additional 5 minutes. Garnish with oregano, if desired.

★ PENNY PINCHER ★ Get more for your money when selecting canned tomatoes! Packed with flavorful extras like green pepper and onions, garlic and even mushrooms, seasoned tomatoes mean fewer ingredients to purchase and prepare.

Chicken & Sausage Skilletini

**Vickie,** Gooseberry Patch

# Tropical Chicken Stir-Fry

This dish is so yummy and cooks up in a jiffy...it's a little taste of the islands! For a sweet end to dinner, I like to serve scoops of orange sherbet and coconut ice cream.

### *Makes 6 servings*

1/4 c. soy sauce
2 T. sugar
1 T. cider vinegar
1 T. catsup
1 T. garlic, minced
1 t. cornstarch
1/2 t. ground ginger
8-oz. can pineapple chunks, drained
    and 1/4 c. juice reserved
2 T. oil
1 lb. boneless, skinless chicken
    breasts, sliced into strips
16-oz. pkg. frozen stir-fry vegetables,
    thawed
cooked rice
Garnish: toasted sliced almonds

In a bowl, mix soy sauce, sugar, vinegar, catsup, garlic, cornstarch, ginger and reserved pineapple juice; set aside. Heat oil in a skillet over medium-high heat. Add chicken; cook and stir for 5 minutes, until nearly done. Add vegetables; cook and stir for 4 minutes, or until cooked through. Stir in pineapple and soy sauce mixture; heat through. Serve over cooked rice; sprinkle with almonds.

★ HOT TIP ★ Toast nuts for extra flavor. Place a single layer of walnuts, pecans or almonds in a skillet. Shake skillet over medium-high heat continually for 5 to 7 minutes, until the nuts turn golden and smell toasty.

**Tropical Chicken Stir-Fry**

**Jo Ann,** Gooseberry Patch

# Chicken Lasagna with Roasted Red Pepper Sauce

There's nothing like a hot pan of lasagna on a cold winter's night! The Roasted Red Pepper Sauce is also great over your favorite noodles.

### Serves 6 to 8

4 c. cooked chicken, finely chopped
2  8-oz. containers chive & onion
   cream cheese
10-oz. pkg. frozen chopped spinach,
   thawed and well drained
1 t. seasoned pepper
3/4 t. garlic salt
9 no-boil lasagna noodles, uncooked
8-oz. pkg. shredded Italian 3-cheese
   blend

Stir together chicken, cream cheese, spinach and seasonings; set aside. Layer a lightly greased 11"x7" baking pan with 1/3 of Roasted Red Pepper Sauce, 3 noodles, 1/3 of chicken mixture and 1/3 of cheese. Repeat layers twice. Place baking pan on a baking sheet. Bake, covered, at 350 degrees for 50 to 55 minutes or until thoroughly heated. Uncover and bake 15 more minutes.

### Roasted Red Pepper Sauce:

12-oz. jar roasted red peppers, drained
16-oz. jar creamy Alfredo sauce
3/4 c. grated Parmesan cheese
1/2 t. red pepper flakes

Process all ingredients in a food processor until smooth, stopping to scrape down sides as needed. Makes 3-1/2 cups.

Chicken Lasagna with Roasted Red Pepper Sauce

**Vickie,** Gooseberry Patch

# Sensational Sirloin Kabobs

Red peppers could also be added for an extra punch of color!

### Serves 6 to 8

1/2 c. lemon-lime flavored soda
1/4 c. soy sauce
3 T. brown sugar, packed
3 T. white vinegar
1/2 t. garlic powder
1/2 t. seasoned salt
1/2 t. garlic pepper seasoning
2 lbs. beef sirloin steak, cut into
   1-1/2 inch cubes
2 green peppers, cubed
2 yellow peppers, cubed
1/2 lb. mushrooms, stems removed
1 pt. cherry tomatoes
6 to 8 skewers
3 c. cooked rice

Combine soda, soy sauce, brown sugar, vinegar and seasonings in a bowl; mix well and set aside. Place steak cubes in a large plastic zipping bag. Add soda mixture, reserving 1/2 cup for basting; seal bag. Refrigerate beef cubes and reserved soda mixture for 8 hours or overnight. Alternately thread steak, peppers, mushrooms and tomatoes onto skewers. Place on a lightly greased grill over high heat. Grill for 10 minutes, or to desired doneness, basting often with reserved marinade during the last 5 minutes of cooking. Serve skewers over cooked rice.

★ SIMPLE INGREDIENT SWAP ★ Try grilling veggies on rosemary skewers for a delicious change. To make the skewers, pull off all but the top leaves from the stem and whittle the opposite end into a point. Slide on vegetables and grill...yummy!

Sensational Sirloin Kabobs

**Vickie,** Gooseberry Patch

# Sweet-Hot Ribeye Steaks

Just add baked potatoes and a big tossed salad for a delicious meal.

*Serves 2 to 4*

1-lb. boneless beef ribeye steak
2 cloves garlic, pressed
2 t. water
2 T. sweet-hot mustard
1 t. fresh rosemary, chopped
1/2 t. fresh thyme, chopped
salt and pepper to taste

Place steak in a shallow dish; set aside. Combine garlic and water in a microwave-safe dish; microwave on high setting for 30 seconds. Stir in mustard and seasonings; brush mixture over both sides of steak. Grill steak over medium-high heat to desired doneness, about 12 minutes for medium. Slice into portions for serving.

**Tricia Schreier,** San Jose, CA

# Grilled Garlic-Stuffed Steaks

Perfect paired with baked potatoes and steamed asparagus.

*Makes 6 servings*

1 T. olive oil
1/4 c. garlic, chopped
1/2 c. green onion, chopped
1/4 t. pepper
2 boneless beef top loin steaks, cut
   2 inches thick

Heat oil in a skillet; add garlic and sauté for 4 to 5 minutes or until tender. Sprinkle in onion; continue to cook for 4 to 5 more minutes until tender. Sprinkle with pepper and set aside. Cut a pocket in each steak; start 1/2 inch from one long side of steak and cut horizontally through the center of the steak to within 1/2 inch of other side. Spread half of garlic mixture inside each steak pocket; secure opening with a metal skewer. Grill, covered, for 22 to 24 minutes or to desired doneness, turning occasionally. Slice steaks crosswise 1/2-inch thick.

Sweet-Hot Ribeye Steaks

**JoAnn,** Gooseberry Patch

# Mexican Lasagna

Use a colorful tablecloth or runner and napkins in vivid hues to give the table a Mexican flair.

*Makes 6 servings*

1 lb. ground beef
16-oz. can refried beans
2 t. dried oregano
1 t. ground cumin
3/4 t. garlic powder
2 c. picante sauce
1-1/2 c. water
9 lasagna noodles, uncooked
16-oz. container sour cream
3/4 c. green onions, thinly sliced
2-1/4 oz. can sliced black olives,
     drained
1 c. shredded Monterey Jack cheese

Brown beef in a large non-stick skillet, stirring until it crumbles; drain and set aside beef. Wipe skillet clean. Return beef to skillet; stir in beans and seasonings. Combine picante sauce and water in a bowl. Pour 1-1/3 cups sauce mixture into a lightly greased 13"x9" baking pan; arrange 3 noodles over sauce mixture. Spread half of beef mixture evenly over noodles; pour one cup remaining sauce mixture over beef mixture and top with 3 more noodles. Spread remaining beef mixture over noodles; top with 3 remaining noodles and spread remaining sauce mixture evenly over noodles. Cover and bake at 350 degrees for 1-1/2 hours. Combine sour cream, onions and olives in a small bowl. Spread sour cream mixture over lasagna and top with cheese. Return to oven and bake 10 more minutes. Let stand 10 minutes before serving.

Mexican Lasagna

**Shay Gardner,** Portland, OR

# Ultimate Cheeseburger Pizza

No need to get out the cutting board... use kitchen shears to chop tomatoes while they are still in the can.

*Makes 4 servings*

1/2 lb. lean ground beef
1/2 t. salt
14-1/2 oz. can whole tomatoes, drained and chopped
1 t. garlic, minced
12-inch prebaked pizza crust
1-1/2 c. shredded Cheddar cheese
1/4 c. green onions, chopped

Brown beef in a skillet over medium-high heat for about 4 minutes, stirring often, until no longer pink; drain and season with salt. Remove from heat and set aside. Stir together tomatoes and garlic; spread evenly over crust. Top with beef, cheese and onions. Place crust directly on oven rack. Bake at 450 degrees for 12 to 14 minutes, until heated through and cheese is melted.

**Katie Majeske,** Denver, PA

# Cheeseburger Cups

When my children were little, this was always a good stand-by for supper. They liked to help by putting the biscuits in the pan. Slices of American cheese may be used, if preferred.

*Makes 5 servings*

1 lb. ground beef
1/2 c. catsup
2 T. brown sugar, packed
1 T. mustard
1-1/2 t. Worcestershire sauce
12-oz. tube refrigerated biscuits
1 c. shredded Cheddar cheese

Brown beef in a skillet over medium heat; drain. Stir in catsup, brown sugar, mustard and Worcestershire sauce; heat through. Press each biscuit into the bottom and up the sides of a greased muffin cup. Spoon beef mixture into cups; top with cheese. Bake at 400 degrees for 15 minutes, or until bubbly and golden.

Ultimate Cheeseburger Pizza

**Beverly Ray,** Brandon, FL

# Chili-Rubbed Steaks

Spice rubs are a great, quick way to give steaks delicious flavor. Add some homemade salsa and you've got a memorable backyard cookout!

*Makes 6 servings*

1 T. ground cumin
2 t. chili powder
1/2 t. salt
1/8 t. pepper
3 boneless sirloin steaks, about
   1/2-inch thick

Mix together seasonings and rub over both sides of steaks; let stand 5 to 10 minutes. Lightly oil grill rack. Grill steaks over medium heat 3 to 5 minutes per side for medium-rare. To serve, slice each steak in half; mound with a generous portion of Chunky Guacamole Salsa. Serve any remaining guacamole on the side.

*Chunky Guacamole Salsa:*

2 avocados, peeled and diced
2 plum tomatoes, chopped
1 jalapeño pepper, chopped
2 T. lime juice
2 T. shallots, chopped
2 T. fresh cilantro, chopped
1-1/2 t. ground cumin
1/2 t. salt
2 T. oil

In a bowl, combine avocados, tomatoes and jalapeño; set aside. In a separate bowl, combine remaining ingredients except oil and mix well. Whisk in oil. Pour over avocado mixture; mix well.

★ FREEZE IT ★ You can freeze mashed, fresh avocado to keep on hand for quick guacamole. Just add 1/2 teaspoon of lime or lemon juice per avocado, mix well, and store in a plastic zipping bag, making sure to remove all the air before sealing. Thaw in the refrigerator before using.

**Chili-Rubbed Steaks**

**LaShelle Brown,** Mulvane, KS

## Idaho Tacos

This is a tasty quick & easy meal to toss together on a busy day. If time is short, you can bake the potatoes in the microwave while you are making the beef mixture.

### Makes 4 servings

4 russet potatoes
1 lb. ground beef
1-1/4 oz. pkg. taco seasoning mix
1/2 c. water
1 c. shredded Cheddar cheese
Garnish: sliced green onions
Optional: salsa

Pierce potatoes several times with a fork. Bake at 400 degrees for 50 to 55 minutes, until fork-tender. With a sharp knife, cut an X in the top of each warm potato; fluff pulp with a fork and set aside. Brown beef in a skillet over medium heat; drain. Stir in seasoning mix and water; bring to a boil. Simmer over low heat for 5 to 7 minutes, stirring occasionally. To serve, top potatoes with beef mixture, cheese, onions and salsa, if desired.

**Andrea Purdon,** Redding, CA

## Horseradish Pot Roast

A tasty pot roast recipe with the added kick of horseradish!

### Serves 12 to 16

4-lb. boneless beef chuck roast
salt and pepper to taste
2 T. oil
1/2 c. onion, chopped
2 c. tomato juice
1/4 c. prepared horseradish
2 T. sherry or water

Sprinkle roast with salt and pepper; brown in hot oil in a Dutch oven. Remove from Dutch oven and set aside; drain all but one tablespoon of drippings. Sauté onion in remaining drippings; add tomato juice, horseradish and sherry or water. Mix well; return meat to pan. Cover; simmer over medium-low heat for 2 to 3 hours or until tender, basting occasionally. Slice meat and serve with sauce.

Idaho Tacos

**Pamela Chorney,** Providence Forge, VA

# Chicken-Pepper Pasta

My husband and I love this dish. The aroma is wonderful!

### *Serves 4 to 6*

6 T. butter
1 onion, chopped
1 red pepper, sliced
1 yellow pepper, sliced
1 t. garlic, minced
3 lbs. boneless, skinless chicken
   breasts, cut into strips
1 t. fresh tarragon, minced
3/4 t. salt
1/4 t. pepper
3/4 c. half-and-half
1 c. shredded mozzarella cheese
1/2 c. grated Parmesan cheese
8-oz. pkg. vermicelli pasta, cooked
Garnish: fresh tarragon

In a skillet, melt butter over medium-high heat until sizzling; stir in onion, peppers and garlic. Cook over medium-high heat until peppers are crisp-tender, 2 to 3 minutes. Remove vegetables from skillet with a slotted spoon and set aside. Add chicken, tarragon, salt and pepper to skillet. Continue cooking, stirring occasionally, until chicken is golden and tender, 7 to 9 minutes. Add vegetables, half-and-half and cheeses to chicken mixture. Reduce heat to medium; cook until cheese has melted, 3 to 5 minutes. Add pasta; toss gently to coat. Garnish with tarragon, if desired. Serve immediately.

**Chicken-Pepper Pasta**

**Dana Thompson,** Delaware, OH

# Country-Fried Steak

The key to cooking these crispy steaks is not to crowd them in the skillet.

### Serves 6 to 8

1-1/2 c. all-purpose flour
1 t. paprika
1 T. salt
1/4 t. pepper
1 c. milk
2 lbs. beef cube steak, cut into
   8 pieces
1/4 c. oil
2.6-oz. pkg. country-style gravy mix

Combine flour and seasonings in a shallow dish; set aside. Add milk to another shallow dish. Dip steaks into milk, then into flour mixture, pressing to coat completely. Heat oil in a large skillet over medium heat. Add steaks in batches; cook for 5 minutes on each side, or until tender and golden, adding oil as needed. Prepare gravy mix according to package directions; spoon over steaks.

**Andrea Heyart,** Aubrey, TX

# Cheddar Meatloaf Roll-Ups

My husband asks for this dish whenever he needs some real comfort food. For the best flavor and texture, chill overnight before baking.

### Makes 6 servings

1-1/2 lbs. ground beef
1/2 c. dry bread crumbs, divided
3 T. barbecue sauce
1 egg, beaten
1/2 t. salt
1/4 t. pepper
1 c. shredded Cheddar cheese
1/4 c. green pepper
2 T. milk

In a large bowl, combine beef, 1/4 cup bread crumbs, barbecue sauce, egg, salt and pepper. Mix well. On a long piece of aluminum foil, pat beef mixture into a 13-inch by 8-inch rectangle. Combine remaining bread crumbs and other ingredients; pat over beef mixture. Roll up beef mixture jelly-roll style, starting on one long side; discard foil. Place in an ungreased 13"x9" glass baking pan. Cover and chill overnight. Uncover; bake at 350 degrees for 30 minutes. Slice to serve.

Country-Fried Steak

**Darlene Nolen,** Whittier, NC

# Steak San Marco

I found this recipe in our local newspaper over twenty years ago. It has become a favorite of our family.

*Serves 4 to 6*

1 lb. beef round steak, sliced into
   thin strips
1 T. oil
1.35-oz. pkg. onion soup mix
28-oz. can diced tomatoes
3 T. cider vinegar
cooked rice

In a skillet over medium heat, brown beef in oil; drain. Add soup mix to beef; mix well. Stir in tomatoes with juice and vinegar. Bring to a low boil and stir until mixed. Reduce heat; cover and simmer for one hour or until beef is tender, stirring occasionally. Serve over cooked rice.

**Teresa Sullivan,** Westerville, OH

# Easy Beef & Mushrooms

A favorite meal spooned over homemade mashed potatoes.

*Makes 2 servings*

1 lb. ground beef
1/2 c. onion, chopped
1 clove garlic, minced
8-oz. pkg. sliced mushrooms
1 T. butter
2 T. all-purpose flour
1/4 t. pepper
1/2 t. salt
1/4 t. paprika
1/2 c. chicken broth
10-3/4 oz. can cream of chicken soup
1 c. sour cream
1-1/2 c. mashed potatoes

Sauté beef, onion, garlic and mushrooms in butter in a large skillet; drain well. Sprinkle flour and seasonings over beef mixture; stir well. Add remaining ingredients except potatoes; mix well and simmer about 30 minutes. Watch carefully to prevent scorching. Serve over potatoes.

Steak San Marco

**Barbara Rannazzisi,** Gainesville, VA

# Mom's Sicilian Pot Roast

Rotini pasta adds to the Sicilian twist of this pot roast...as do the other Italian flavors. Delicious served over hot cooked rice or savory mashed potatoes too.

### Serves 8 to 10

2 T. garlic-flavored olive oil
4-lb. rolled rump beef roast
2 28-oz. cans whole tomatoes
2 8-oz. cans Italian tomato sauce
1/2 c. water
1 T. garlic, minced
1 t. dried oregano
1 t. dried basil
1 t. dried parsley
1-1/2 t. salt
1/2 t. pepper
Optional: 1/4 c. all-purpose flour,
   2 c. hot water
cooked rotini pasta
Optional: fresh basil sprigs

Heat oil in a Dutch oven over medium heat; brown roast on all sides. Drain; add tomatoes with juice, tomato sauce, water, garlic and seasonings. Bring to a boil; reduce heat to medium-low. Cover and simmer for 2-1/2 hours or until tender, turning occasionally. Remove roast to a cutting board; cut into serving-size slices and return to sauce in pan. Simmer, uncovered, for 30 more minutes. If sauce is not thick enough, combine flour and water, stirring until dissolved. Gradually stir flour mixture into sauce, a little at a time, until sauce thickens. To serve, place cooked pasta on a large platter; top with sauce and sliced roast. Garnish with fresh oregano sprigs, if desired.

**Mom's Sicilian Pot Roast**

**Alma Meyers,** Guernsey, WY

# Quick Salisbury Steak

Add a side of mashed potatoes for a hearty, filling dinner.

### Makes 4 servings

1 lb. ground beef
1-1/2 oz. pkg. onion soup mix
2 eggs, beaten
2  10-3/4 oz. cans golden mushroom
    soup

In a large bowl, combine beef, soup mix and eggs; mix well and form into 4 patties. Place patties in an ungreased 13"x9" baking pan; cover with soup. Bake at 350 degrees for 35 minutes, or until patties are no longer pink in the center.

**Lisa Robason,** Corpus Christi, TX

# Jalapeño-Bacon Cheese Steak

Perfect for summertime grilling! We serve this with borracho beans, Spanish rice and cornbread.

### Serves 6 to 8

2 lbs. ground beef chuck
1-3/4 c. soft bread crumbs
3/4 c. beef broth
2 eggs, beaten
1 T. salt
1-1/2 t. pepper
8-oz. pkg. shredded Cheddar cheese
8 slices bacon, diced and crisply
    cooked
4 green onions, sliced
2 jalapeño peppers, seeded and
    chopped

Place beef in a large bowl; set aside. In a separate bowl, combine bread crumbs and beef broth; mix well. Add bread crumb mixture, eggs and seasonings to beef; mix gently and form into 8 patties. Grill patties over medium heat for about 8 minutes on each side. May also place patties on an ungreased baking sheet and bake at 300 degrees for 30 minutes. Top with cheese, bacon, onions and peppers during the last few minutes of cooking.

**Quick Salisbury Steak**

**Cris Goode,** Mooresville, IN

# Deep-Dish Pizza

This is the pizza recipe my family would always make on pizza nights when I was growing up. These days it's an often-requested favorite around here!

### Serves 6 to 8

1 lb. ground beef
1/2 c. onion, chopped
2 cloves garlic, minced
2  8-1/2 oz. pkgs. pizza crust mix
14-oz. jar pizza sauce
4-oz. can sliced mushrooms, drained
1/4 c. green pepper, chopped
3.8-oz. can sliced black olives, drained
2-1/2 c. shredded mozzarella cheese

In a skillet over medium heat, brown beef with onion and garlic until beef is no longer pink. Drain; set aside. Meanwhile, prepare pizza crust according to package directions. Transfer to a greased 13"x9" baking pan, pressing dough halfway up sides of the pan. Pierce dough several times with a fork. Bake at 425 degrees for 5 minutes; remove from oven. Cover with pizza sauce; layer with beef mixture and remaining ingredients. Bake, uncovered, at 425 degrees for 20 to 25 minutes, until bubbly and cheese is melted.

★ TIME-SAVING SHORTCUT ★ You may be able to purchase fresh, unbaked pizza dough from your favorite pizza shop. It's also often found in the refrigerator case at the supermarket.

**Deep-Dish Pizza**

**Kay Marone,** Des Moines, IA

# Flaky Beef Turnovers

Be sure to cut the potatoes into very small pieces so they'll be cooked by the time the pastry shells are golden.

### Makes 6 turnovers

6-oz. boneless beef ribeye steak,
   coarsely chopped
1 potato, peeled and diced
3 T. onion soup mix
2 T. catsup
1 t. Worcestershire sauce
1 T. fresh parsley, chopped
10-oz. pkg. puff pastry shells, thawed

Combine steak, potatoes, soup mix, catsup, Worcestershire sauce and parsley in a large bowl. On a lightly floured surface, roll out each pastry shell into a 7-inch circle. Fill each pastry circle with 1/4 cup beef mixture; lightly brush edges of pastry with water. Fold circles in half; seal edges with the tines of a fork. With a knife tip, cut several slits in the top of each turnover; place on a lightly greased baking sheet. Bake at 400 degrees for 20 to 25 minutes, until golden.

**Suzanne Bayorgeon,** Norfolk, NY

# Cheeseburger Macaroni

If you're headed out afterward to a ball game or to the movies, you'll love this supper recipe...it's kid-friendly, quick & easy!

### Serves 4 to 6

1 lb. ground beef
2-1/4 c. water
1/2 c. catsup
1 t. mustard
2 c. elbow macaroni, uncooked
12-oz. pkg. pasteurized process cheese
   spread, cubed

Brown beef in a large skillet over medium heat. Drain; add water, catsup and mustard. Bring to a boil and stir in uncooked macaroni. Reduce heat to medium-low; cover and simmer for 8 to 10 minutes, until macaroni is tender. Add cheese; stir until melted.

**Flaky Beef Turnovers**

**Heidi Maurer,** Garrett, IN

# Hunter's Pie

My 3-year-old son Hunter loves this and my 8-year-old son Luke does too... but without the beans!

*Makes 4 servings*

1 lb. roast beef, cooked and cubed
12-oz. jar beef gravy
16-oz. pkg. frozen classic mixed
　vegetables, thawed
9-inch deep-dish pie crust, baked
11-oz. tube refrigerated bread sticks

Combine all ingredients except pie crust and bread sticks; spread into pie crust. Arrange unbaked bread sticks on top, criss-cross style. Bake at 350 degrees for 20 minutes, or until heated through and bread sticks are golden.

★ SAVVY SIDE ★ **A delicious no-fuss side...tuck some roasted vegetables into the oven along with a main-dish casserole. Toss peeled, sliced veggies with a little olive oil and spread on a baking sheet. Bake at 350 degrees, stirring occasionally, for 15 to 25 minutes, until tender and golden.**

Hunter's Pie

**INDEX**

## Melts & Wraps

## Salads

## Sandwiches & Subs

## Soups, Stews & Chilis

# U. S. to Metric Recipe Equivalents

## Volume Measurements

¼ teaspoon ........................... 1 mL
½ teaspoon ........................... 2 mL
1 teaspoon ........................... 5 mL
1 tablespoon = 3 teaspoons......... 15 mL
2 tablespoons = 1 fluid ounce....... 30 mL
¼ cup............................... 60 mL
⅓ cup............................... 75 mL
½ cup = 4 fluid ounces............. 125 mL
1 cup = 8 fluid ounces............. 250 mL
2 cups = 1 pint = 16 fluid ounces .. 500 mL
4 cups = 1 quart........................... 1 L

## Weights

1 ounce................................ 30 g
4 ounces............................. 120 g
8 ounces............................. 225 g
16 ounces = 1 pound.................. 450 g

## Baking Pan Sizes

### Square

8x8x2 inches............. 2 L = 20x20x5 cm
9x9x2 inches.......... 2.5 L = 23x23x5 cm

### Rectangular

13x9x2 inches.......... 3.5 L = 33x23x5 cm

### Loaf

9x5x3 inches............. 2 L = 23x13x7 cm

### Round

8x1-1/2 inches............. 1.2 L = 20x4 cm
9x1-1/2 inches............. 1.5 L = 23x4 cm

## Recipe Abbreviations

t. = teaspoon          ltr. = liter
T. = tablespoon        oz. = ounce
c. = cup               lb. = pound
pt. = pint             doz. = dozen
qt. = quart            pkg. = package
gal. = gallon          env. = envelope

## Oven Temperatures

300˚ F ............................... 150° C
325˚ F................................. 160° C
350˚ F................................. 180° C
375˚ F................................. 190° C
400˚ F ............................... 200° C
450˚ F................................. 230° C

## Kitchen Measurements

A pinch = ⅛ tablespoon
1 fluid ounce = 2 tablespoons
3 teaspoons = 1 tablespoon
4 fluid ounces = ½ cup
2 tablespoons = ⅛ cup
8 fluid ounces = 1 cup
4 tablespoons = ¼ cup
16 fluid ounces = 1 pint
8 tablespoons = ½ cup
32 fluid ounces = 1 quart
16 tablespoons = 1 cup
16 ounces net weight = 1 pound
2 cups = 1 pint
4 cups = 1 quart
4 quarts = 1 gallon